Books in the
On Becoming Series

Birthwise
Babywise
Babywise Two
Pre-Toddlerwise
Toddlerwise
Pottywise for Toddlers
Preschoolwise
Childwise
Preteenwise
Teenwise

ON BECOMING
PRE-TODDLERWISE

FROM BABYHOOD TO TODDLERHOOD
(Parenting Your Twelve to Eighteen Month Old)

GARY EZZO, M.A.
ROBERT BUCKNAM, M.D.

PARENT-WISE SOLUTIONS, INC.

Parent-Wise Solutions Publishing
(A Division of The Charleston Publishing Group, Inc.)

ON BECOMING PRETODDLERWISE
Parenting Your Twelve to Eighteen Month Old

International Standard Book Number

ISBN-13 978-1-932740-11-0

Printed in the United States of America

Parent-Wise Solutions, Inc.
P.O. Box 54
Louisiana, MO 63353

www.parentwisesolutions.com

12 11 10 09 - 5 4 3 2 1

Dedicated To:
Harold and Nancy

We forge friendships in youth because of locality,
during midlife because of convenience,
in old age because of the meaning of life.
The first is the right place, the second is the right time,
the third is the right purpose.

ACKNOWLEDGMENTS

We are of course, grateful for the assistance given by many associates from the Charleston area who made this book and series possible. Where would we be without our medical advisors and friends? We wish to thank Dr. Robert Turner for providing his oversight specifically dealing with matters pertaining to pediatric neurology and Dr. Alan Furness for his contribution to the section on dental care. We also wish to thank the many Moms and Dads in our study groups who provided responses, e-mails and questions that greatly contributed to the practical side of this book.

From outside our geographic locality came the contribution of Cyndi Bird who provided assistance with the nap and nighttime sleep chapter. Of course, good editors are responsible for the book's readability. We wish to acknowledge our dear friend and long term associate, Carla Link for her editorial contribution and parenting insights. Her comments are always valued and appreciated. Last but not least is a big thank you to Paige Hunter who assisted us in putting the finishing touches on this manuscript.

CONTENTS

Preface

C hange! It seems to be a way of life for parents. In our rapidly expanding, knowledge-based society where technology changes everyday, new innovations impact life styles and the way people learn. Parenting curriculums, once designed to cover large blocks of developmental time are less effective today than years gone by. Precision teaching with concise thoughts for specific age ranges seems to be the way of educational life. Our newest curriculum reflects these changes.

The communication and dissemination of early childhood principles are easily and naturally divided into four developmental stages, starting at birth and going to thirty-six months. Each stage represents new growth transitions requiring parents to accommodate the changes taking place as their child's grows. Our early childhood curriculum now include:

Stage One: Birth to 5 Months ~ On Becoming Babywise
Stage Two: 5 to 12 Months ~ On Becoming Babywise II
Stage Three: 12 to 18 Months ~ On Becoming Pretoddlerwise
Stage Four: 18-36 Months ~ On Becoming Toddlerwise

We continue this series where *Babywise II* left off. During the next 180 days, the newly emerging walking, talking, exploring child begins a developmental metamorphosis from babyhood to toddlerhood. This means the challenges successfully accomplished a few months ago give way to new abilities and challenges as your pretoddler's mind and world expands exponentially. As mealtime and waketime activities become more complex, parenting strategies will have to adjust to properly accommodate your child's expanding world of discovery. *On Becoming Pretoddlerwise* was written to prepares parents for the hectic, fast moving, exciting and fatiguing toddler years.

As in the case of all everything we have previously written, *On Becoming Pretoddlerwise* will provide trustworthy ideas and workable solutions, but not every possible application. As you read through each lesson, it's vital that you think in terms of principle. Understanding a 'principle' of parenting, derived from your own hierarchy of beliefs and values, is a greater asset than just having a list of 'how-to' answers. Principle parenting is wisdom parenting extended. Thanks for joining us in the next adventure of parenting.

Robert Bucknam, M.D.

Introduction

❦

Between the ages of twelve and eighteen months, a pretoddler is on a one-way track to the future. This is a growth phase made-up of tiny daily and weekly transitions linking the babyhood days with the up coming toddlerhood months. It is a time when your child is in neither. We wish we could title this series "Nine Easy Visits." Unfortunately, that would not be descriptive of the unfolding days ahead. This transitional period will be anything but easy, especially for first-time parents. That is because the speed in which your pretoddler will grow physically and intellectually is staggering and can catch any parent off guard.

Our goal is putting this book together is related to helping parents acquire useful knowledge that will prepare them for what lies around the next corner – the reality of toddlerhood. Right now there are plenty of new skills to master and new behaviors for parents to understand. Helping you make wise decisions on behalf of your child now and in the future is one of our primary goals in this presentation. The more parents understand the various transitions, the more confident they become in managing their child's world.

Where are we Going?

It's beneficial to the reader to have a general road map of where our journey through the pretoddler months will take us. We divided the book into for general visits, each with their own subchapters. In our first visit, we address the challenges that are part of a pretoddler's unfolding world. We will also look at some trustworthy goals and objectives for this transition period. We conclude with a challenge to fathers. What does it mean to Mom and child when Dad is fully engaged in the parenting process? Everything wonderful!

Food and nutrition are the primary topics of discussion in the second visit. We'll cover the fundamentals of dietary change and discuss some potential food challenges that often accompany this phase of growth. We close our visit with a thorough discussion of naps and nighttime sleep transitions.

We then move to Visit Three and waketime activities. Here, our conversation turns to one of the most important pretoddler and toddler parenting strategies, the funnel factor. While we cannot provide a 100% guarantee relating to outcome, we can promise that when applied consistently, this parenting strategy will lead to less frustration for Mom, Dad and child and many more moments of family harmony. Visit Three is all about how to rightly manage your child's play environment and the impact that will have on his ability to learn and gain age-appropriate self-control.

From there we move to Visit Four and age-appropriate forms of correction. The preventative side of training, doing those things that help reduce the need for correction, is the primary emphasis of our discussion. But human nature, being what it is, means correction in the life of your pretoddler will still be necessary. What will that look like in your home? We concluded this visit with our topic pool section, a collection of relevant topics of common interest that are directly related to your everyday experience as a parent of a pretoddler.

On the technical side of this book, it is our custom to use

the masculine references of "he," "his," and "him" in most cases. The principles of this book will of course work just as well with raising daughters. Further, we do not claim or insist that this is all the information you will need to raise a pretoddler. It would take volumes more knowledge than we possess. Therefore, parents guided by their own convictions have the ultimate responsibility to research parenting philosophies available today and make an informed decision as to what is best for their family. Please keep in mind as you work through the content that unless otherwise noted, when using the term "pretoddlers", we are specifically focusing on the ages between twelve to eighteen months. We know many rewarding experiences are just around the corner as you move into this exciting phase. Enjoy your pretoddler.

Gary Ezzo

Visit One

Managing Your Assets ~ Minimizing Your Liabilities

Chapter One

A Bridge to Somewhere

Y ou help your son blow out his first birthday candle and Great Aunt Lilly proclaims, "He's a toddler now!" Not so fast! The period between twelve and eighteen months places a child on a one-way bridge to the future. Infancy is a thing of the past and toddlerhood is straight ahead. A baby still? Not really, but neither is he a toddler and that is the key to understanding this phase of growth. Take a couple of photos because the child leaving infancy will not resemble the child entering toddlerhood six months down the road. This is a period of metamorphosis when his potential for learning seems limitless, his budding curiosity unquenchable and his energy level never seems to diminish.

This is also a period of great *exchange*: baby food is exchanged for table food; the highchair for booster seat; finger feeding replaced with spoon; babbling sounds will transition to speaking, the first unsteady steps are conquered by strides of confidence, and the list goes on. Moving at a lightening pace and equipped with a mind of his own, your pretoddler is driven towards a new level of independence. Whether you're ready or not his natural inclination and challenge of "*I do myself*" will become increasingly apparent, not to mention frustrating.

The emerging pretoddler is acutely aware of self, although

at twelve months of age he is not fully absorbed in the self-importance of *me, myself and I*. (Hang on, that blessing of his nature will show up around twenty months of age.) Try taking something away and a scream of protest is likely. Remove him from a dangerous object and his curiosity lures him right back. His favorite foods suddenly become not-so-favorite and in a few months "No!" will become his default word whether he understands the question or not.

The natural inclination within pretoddlers towards independence is very strong yet, unpredictable. He is always in motion and not easily restrained, directed or controlled, but he needs to be! Boundaries will be tested, rules understood as suggestions, and curiosity will become a force to be reckoned with. How will you meet these unfolding challenges? That is the big question. The answer begins with understanding the various growth transitions of the next one hundred and eighty days of your pretoddler's life.

THE GROWTH FACTOR

No matter how well-read you become on the topic of child development, how many classes you attend or how often you search the Internet, there is one fact to remember: your pretoddler is different than all others. No child has the same variables of influence on him or her as the one found in your home. Thus, as your pretoddler grows, so also must you grow in understanding — an understanding that weds his unfolding world with your specific interests and objectives.

These are the *variable* factors influencing growth and the attainment of life skills. The differences in each family will not allow for cookie-cutter solutions. For example, a stay-at-home mom faces different challenges than a mom working outside the home. In addition, health factors, job transfers, even another pregnancy adds more variables. Does that mean all is hopeless? Certainly not! Principles and goals do not change, but applications will be adjusted to meet the unique needs of your family.

Yet, at the same time parents can find some comfort in knowing every child possesses similar growth patterns as other children. These form the *constant* factors of development. Inherent within these factors is predictability. Let's look at a few that will require your attention.

In our previous book, *"Babywise II" (Parenting Your Six to Twelve Month Old)* we looked at two processes that dominate. These processes are growth and learning which are activities that are *interdependent* but are not *interchangeable*. Growth refers to the biological process of life whereas learning refers to the mental process. Both growth and learning start with building blocks that are progressive, meaning each stage of development depends on the successful completion of the previous stage. What are some of the biological growth factors affecting your pretoddler?

Growth Rates

Your baby's growth rate is one factor to beware of. Babies grow rapidly during the first year but their growth slows considerably after that. That means the rapid weight gain common during infancy is replaced with steady, but significantly slower weight gain during the pretoddler and toddler phases. At six months of age, your baby probably doubled his birth weight, but the feat is unlikely to occur again for another two or three years. Growth in height is also affected. Pretoddlers on average slow down significantly, adding only ten percent in height to their physical stature between ages one and three. These combined factors explain why a pretoddler's nutritional needs level off. The child simply does not require as much food to sustain his growth pace. (We'll speak more about the nutritional transitions in Visit Two.)

Teething

On average, a one-year-old will have acquired six teeth, four upper incisors and two lower. The remaining fourteen "baby teeth" will come in by his third birthday. Baby teeth are eventually replaced by a second set of thirty-two "permanent teeth" Sometime between twelve and twenty months, your pretoddler's first molars will break through, creating temporary discomfort. (The final molars appear by thirty-six months.) The sequence of *how* the temporary teeth erupt is usually of more concern to a pediatrician than *when*. The lower teeth should erupt first, then the upper set. If the sequence is reversed it often affects the alignment of temporary and permanent teeth. There is not much a parent can do about this condition except to be aware of the probable need for correction during middle childhood.

Stay mindful of the need for early dental care because baby teeth are at risk for decay. If you haven't already, we encourage you to set up your pretoddler's first dental appointment. Baby teeth, although temporary, are important and early screening along with preventive care goes a long way in protecting your child now and in the future. We expand on dental care in our Chapter Twelve.

Walking

A big change in your pretoddler's life, (and yours) comes with the transition from crawling to walking. This normally occurs between ten and eighteen months of age. In times past, clinicians referred to the early steps as 'toddling'. From this description the label 'toddler' became popular. However, much more is involved in toddlerhood than mastering the skill of walking.

A child's new-found mobility is nothing new because months ago he began creeping, then crawling, standing, and then walking from object to object. One day it happened — he took his first step. From that point forward, his world and yours changed. Walking is a developmental milestone because it marks a new era of independence. His little feet can now take him where his mind wants to go and that means, when he is on the go, you're probably not going to be far behind.

Walking will require more direct parental supervision because mobility increases a child's contact with his world. Walking opens doors of opportunity and new areas of interest, exploration and adventure. But all is not rosy because now he is able to walk into mischief and trouble. As a crawler you knew his range of exploration. As a walker, you must keep your eye on him constantly since his ability and resolve to get from here to there far exceeds his judgment of caution and safety. The walking, talking, exploring pretoddler and toddler demands his mother's time, energy, and patience more than any other phase of growth. It is also a time when clashes of the 'will' abound, for the walking-about toddler is in the process of not only testing his legs and hands but also trying new experiences with his mind.

If left to himself, unhindered by moral and safety concerns, this little person could empty a bookshelf in minutes, connect with Hong Kong on Dad's wireless phone, drink from the bird-bath, splash his hands in the toilet, drain the last sips of the beverage left on the coffee table, flee the kitchen with a table knife in hand, or take a nap in the dog house — which, after everything else, would be a positive thing!

Ah yes, the mobile pretoddler. There is no question that a pretoddler's mom is a tired mom, and for good reason. The emotional and physical energy needed to supervise an energy-packed tot can take down the most physically-fit mom. If your pretoddler happens to be a boy, add fifty percent more energy into the equation. Yes, it is true, never so beautiful does this child look to his weary parents as he does when he closes his eyes at night in sleep.

FACTORS OF LEARNING

Where biological maturation refers to changes in physical capacities tied to genetic cues, learning signifies changes resulting from interaction with one's environment. For the most part, learning is brought about by parental influence and instruction. Allowing a child to progress in an orderly manner in his or her new and expanding world greatly enhances healthy learning. Add to these are other influences on learning including the child's temperament, the presence or absence of siblings, parental resolve, the purpose for training, the method of instruction, and reinforcement of parental training are some to consider.

Like adults, children relate new experiences in the context of what they already know and understand. Learning is progressive, built on fragments of meaningful data. But the pieces, like a puzzle must be assembled correctly to make sense.

For example, pushing a jack-in the-box off the edge of his highchair tray may cause it to burst open. Another push off the highchair does nothing. Such random action does not provide the child understanding as to what makes the 'Jack' jump out of the box, so the true joy of discovery is lost. Only after careful study, demonstration, and moments spent fiddling with the box does the curious pretoddler learn to appreciate the cause and effect of his actions. The jack-in-the-box jumps out after he turns the crank. In this way he has correctly assembled the fragments of data and purposeful learning has taken place.

But there is more going on here. Your pretoddler has not simply learned how to open the Jack-in-the Box for the moment, but also acquired a type of mechanical logic that is transferred to other toys. It's this logic that aids reasoning skills in the future.

Routine and orderly transitions at each stage of a pretoddler's development aids the marriage between new information or new experiences and the ability to understand them. On the other hand, learning is negatively impacted by random activity. For example, a pretoddler rummaging through a cabinet, discarding its contents in the dog's dish and then scampers into the living room when he hears the TV come on, is certainly random activity, but has there been any beneficial learning?

This type of activity is called 'amusement'. The word. 'Muse' means 'to think' and the prefix 'a' means 'without', therefore, the definition of 'amusement' means 'without thinking'. While some play will be 'amusing', as a parent you need to monitor how much of your child's play falls into this category. What is your pretoddler's day like? If there is no routine in his day that allows for some structured learning time, then his day will just be filled with amusement. Is he still doing playpen time? It continues to provide a wonderful opportunity for some structured learning time during the day.

Since learning comes in progressive stages, training should take place in the same way. For this reason, parents should provide their child with a learning environment that matches information with understanding. And that is the key to pretoddler and toddler training. His learning is dependent on the environment you create. This is more simple than you might think and far more beautiful than a kitchen covered with pots, pans, and toys strewn everywhere.

WHAT DO PARENTS NEED TO KNOW?

Where does confidence come from? Confidence comes in part from knowing what to expect at each stage of a child's development. As stated earlier, the period between twelve and eighteen months of age is a bridge linking babyhood to toddlerhood. The child is in transition. Transition means 'change'. Sometimes change can make parents and children uncomfortable because it moves both out of their comfort zone or habits of familiarity. For those of you who have put into practice the principles learned in "*Babywise*," the good news comes from the confidence of knowing you are not entering a totally new arena of parenting during the next six months but extending the training that you are already familiar with. You are already familiar with the three activities of your baby's day: feeding time, waketime and naptime. These three continue to be primary in your pretoddler's day but now they're going to look a little different because of the growth transitions. For example:

Feeding Time

The mealtime transitions during this phase are many. Consider these changes:

• Your child may start the pretoddler phase being fed pureed foods and by the end of this phase is capable of feeding himself the food the rest of the family is eating.

- At the beginning of this phase he may be drinking formula from a bottle or nursing, and by the end of the phase he is drinking whole milk from a sippy cup.

- At a year of age you are still carrying him to his meals, but in six months he is capable of coming on his own when called.

- He may start in a highchair and end the phase in a booster seat.

- He may start with his own dinnertime because he can't wait to eat later with the rest of the family but by the end of the transition he is joining the family at regular mealtimes.

Naptime

The nap transitions are fairly simple. Pretoddlers go from two naps or (two naps and a catnap) down to one nap. However, this impacts another dimension of your child's day, that being *waketime*.

Waketime

Increased waketime corresponds to less naptime. Additional waketime provides more time for interaction with siblings and parents. It also creates new learning and training opportunities, not to mention the fun-filled challenge associated with your pretoddler's emerging '*self*'. Increased mobility and waketime equals increased opportunities for trouble! As a result, parental guidance takes on a greater sense of urgency. This is because a pretoddler is too young to reason with but too mobile to be left alone. He needs loving supervision and guidance.

Chapter Two
Setting the Right Goals

The world of change must at times seem completely baffling to a pretoddler. His newly acquired skill of walking does not develop in sync with a required level of self-control necessary to be left alone. As soon as he can move, he believes he can do it all and when he finds out he can't, frustration will show. This challenge in development creates numerous issues for parents because in this season of transition there is a disparity between the child's mobility and his understanding of what is safe and best for his welfare. This disparity will continue right through the toddler years. Thus, into the scene steps Mom and Dad looking for the balance between granting their pretoddler freedom to discover with setting appropriate limitations out of health and safety concerns.

The Achievable Goal

Understand that in the context of pretoddler parenting there is an over-arching goal that is achievable and worthy of pursuit. This goal will not leave you frazzled at the end of day or wondering if you or your child is missing something along the way. It is a strategy that can guide you through the entire pretoddler transition. Here is what we're suggesting. Over the next six months:

Do not worry about gaining ground with your pretoddler, (behaviorally speaking), but rather focus on not losing ground. By not losing ground you are actually gaining ground. Manage your assets and avoid creating any new liabilities.

Think of it from an investment viewpoint. You already invested a great amount time and effort into training your pre-toddler. That is why you are now enjoying good nighttime sleep habits, contentment during playpen time, and a child that communicates through signing words rather than screaming. Your pretoddler is already reasonably respectful of your basic boundaries. Add to these healthy wake and mealtime activi-ties and you can begin to see why these investments are worth protecting. These are behavioral assets.

Your goal over the next six months is to protect these assets by managing them while avoiding the creation of any new behavioral liabilities. When speaking of behavioral liabilities we are referring to any behavior or skill that was once achieved and a normal part of your child's day that begins to slip away, or new behavior that is constantly calling for correction. Here are some general examples of what we mean.

Example One

Your twelve-month-old has been sleeping wonderfully through the night but suddenly begins to wake at 5:00 am rather than his normal 7:00 am. Instead of working to under-stand why the child is waking early, you decide there is nothing that can be done about it and therefore surrender to a 5:00 am wake-up call. This change now impacts his total sleep creating a morning fussy time that wasn't there a few days ago. Instead of managing your child's healthy nighttime sleep habits, you took a draw on your investment and lost a portion of your assets, (and created a new liability).

Example Two

How about the playpen? Last week your pretoddler loved his playpen time entertaining himself contently for thirty minutes or more, twice a day. Now he finds the playpen undesirable and lets you know through his screaming. What will you do? He certainly is not ready for 'room time'! So, do you give in and put the playpen away? What then? His ability to play by himself created by the friendly and safe environment of the playpen is lost. Do you really want to give up that asset or would you rather *manage* it?

Example Three

One day your child decides he no longer wants his favorite foods. What will you do? If you give into every preference all the time a mealtime liability will be created. In this case the joy of pleasant mealtimes are displaced with the unpleasantness of a potential picky eater.

EASIER SAID THAN DONE?

We already established that plenty of new challenges come with your child's march toward toddlerhood. Hopefully you will face these new experiences with confidence, wisdom, and understanding. But what happens when challenges come to those foundational assets already in place? Here are four words to help you through the various and unexpected bumps in the road like the three we just described above. Think on these words.

Unpredictable

Unpredictable means unable to foresee or expect; something not according to plan.' Count on it! During this transition *unpredictability* is something that is unfortunately very predictable.

For example, one day Zoey loves her playpen and the next two days she doesn't. For the next two weeks she loves it again. One day she loves her green beans, the next day they are a source of torment and anguish.

Parents stay mindful of this fact. You are going into a phase of "unpredictability". It will be a way of life for the next six months at least. But the good new is, you have a safety net — the asset of your daily routine. Stick with it and repeat the following word to yourself over and over again, "persevere".

Persevere

Persevere is to persist or remain committed to a purpose or task in the face of obstacles. With all the changes taking place, your pretoddler begins to expand his world of preference, likes and dislikes. When it comes to the things that matter to you, persevere with your goals especially during those unpredictable moments when you're not sure what to do. Perseverance has its rewards and your pretoddler is the benefactor of them. Persevering sees you through those moments of discouragement when you think all is lost. Keep going. Tomorrow all can be regained and with compound interest in your favor.

Concrete

Here is another word representing an important pretoddler concept. Concrete means tangible, touchable and viewable. In early childhood education, concepts that can be communicated or aided by concrete examples speed the process of understanding. In a discussion with one of our consulting Moms, this point was made clear as she described a playpen incident with thirteen-month-old Brody. Disturbed by being put in the playpen, little Brody sounded his protest until Mom placed the timer so Brody could see it. For whatever reason, the protest stopped and for days after little Brody was very happy in his playpen. Pretoddlers and toddlers relate to concrete objects. Sometimes just seeing an item satisfies them. It also means the more you can show your child what to do, the faster he learns.

Context

Context is to understand the circumstances in which an event occurs. We have all heard it said, "Let's keep things in context." You cannot parent with confidence without understanding the relevancy of this concept. Responding to the context of any situation does not mean we suspend our goals or plans but that we apply judgment and make wise decisions in the most appropriate way given present circumstances.

During the pretoddler phase, parenting beliefs and goals are easily challenged, refined and adjusted. Parenting a pretoddler and toddler is a time when parental idealism often surrenders to reality. You know your goals for the next six months, but sometimes, unexpected twists, turns, and bumps in the road come your way. As a Mom or Dad you cannot expect all things to go according to plan or expectation. Parenting doesn't work that way. Context is what allows you to achieve freedom in the decision-making process without compromising your long-range goals or objectives.

For example, you might offer a new dinner food that is met with strong protest. Instead of insisting on 'winning today at all cost', consider the context of the situation and the developmental age of your child, or the already present challenges of the day. Maybe tomorrow is a better day to offer this new food and maybe lunch is the better time to do so.

Chapter Three
A Few Words for Fathers

It's a fact. A child's personality is shaped by the many influences of early childhood. As it relates to parenting, Mom and Dad are the only world a pretoddler knows and thus their influence is unmatched! But what does that world look like? A father shares a common responsibility with Mom for creating the nurturing environment of the home. And no other foundational truth has as much influence on a child's sense of security as does Mom and Dad's relationship with each other. If nurturing doesn't take place there, within that relationship, it will not fully take place in parenting.

One of the greatest gifts parents can pass onto their children is a beautiful and ongoing demonstration of love for each other. This starts with a mutual commitment to invest, grow and maintain a healthy husband-wife relationship. When there is harmony in the marriage, there is stability within the family. That is the bottom line and the place where it all begins and where it all ends.

When the marital relationship is made beautiful, what impressionable child would not want to be part of the family? When two are mysteriously and beautifully united in marriage, what child would not seek the comfort and security of that togetherness? The mantra for successful parenting begins with this truth — the best years of your parenting will flow out of the best years of your marriage. Protect and celebrate it together because great marriages produce great parents. When Dad is on board with this truth, he is on board with parenting.

ALL THAT DAD CAN DO

The effective father is first and foremost an effective husband and there are some very wonderful things he can and should do to demonstrate servant leadership in his home. Servant leadership is sacrificial, caring, honoring, and reaffirms those timeless words that rise above all else, those first words serving as a pledge to the future "I love you." What might this look like in your home? Here are a few suggestions for Dads that send the right message to Mom and your children.

Showing Honor

If we trace the breakdown in fatherhood, it tends to begin at the point when a husband fails to honor Mom as his wife and not just as the mother of his children. There is no substitute for a husband who routinely does things that demonstrate a loving commitment to his wife. This could be through acts of service, (doing something that you know she is going to appreciate), giving her undivided attention, or gracing her with words of encouragement. Equally important is making sure that going on a date night once a week happens. It may be a couple of hours over dinner or a visit to a local coffee shop. Such times have value because it is taking your wife out of her role of mother-hood and celebrating her first role as a wife and friend. The best gift any father can give his children is a visible demonstration that Mom is the most important woman in the world.

Speak Words of Appreciation

Affirmation is a valued gift a mother never grows tired of receiving. These are words expressing Dad's appreciation for the special little things that makes his home a sanctuary of love; the great meal he finds on the dinner table or the joy of his children, which is often a reflection of what Mom has done during the day. Dad can start with "thank you" and build from there. Sincere words of encouragement are gifts that every woman appreciate and they are words not soon forgotten.

Like-Mindedness

No dad has the luxury of a single job. When he leaves his day-job he heads home for the most important vocation of his life, that being a husband and a father. This means more than just going home and changing a diaper now and then. It means sitting down with his wife and asking questions that can help him stay connected to what is going on in Mom's day.

Possibly you might consider making Dad the "Why Manager" of the home. Rather than just accepting "This is what moms do," a husband should routinely seek to understand how and why she came to her parenting decisions during the day. This is not an intrusion on Mom's judgment, but a way that will help both Mom and Dad stay accountable to their goals and beliefs. Work on having a consistent time to discuss what is going on in the family, which keeps Dad informed and affords opportunity for Mom to hear a second opinion. Being like-minded provides a mutually agreed starting point. By that we mean, when parenting challenges do come your way, you are not left wondering in that moment, what you believe as a couple. Rather, like-mindedness has you working together towards solutions within the boundaries of what you already know and embrace.

Knowing Why

Remember, parenting is a team effort. A mom can't do it alone nor does she really want to. This is one good reason why couples should continue to set aside a few minutes each day to talk through challenges or changes relating to the little person in the home. This will make for some great Couch-time conversation.

Women appreciate a husband who is willing to participate in the 'knowledge' side of parenting. It would be helpful for Dad to know his son's routine. Try taking your pretoddler for a day, starting at breakfast, through naps and into dinner time. This experience not only gives your wife the gift of time, but more importantly, it gives you the gift of understanding of what it is like to be 'Mom' every day. Husbands who care in the little things care in the big ones even more.

But cultivating Dad's support begins with Mom keeping him informed. We can tell you from experience that when a man thinks all is going well at home, he has a tendency and maybe a willingness to stay blissfully ignorant of any challenges. Mom, you need to keep Dad informed if you want his support. Dad will listen better to what you are trying to share with him if done so in a calm manner and not in the heat of a crisis or immediately as he walks through the door. Keeping Dad informed really is all part of a mutual partnership to manage your child's positive behaviors and minimize the things that can lead to negative ones.

Seeking Understanding
True love does not default to judgment, but first seeks understanding. Not every day will end up being the perfect day when Dad walks through the door. He may walk into a chaotic situation without knowing what has been going on earlier that day. He sees his toddler son pulling papers off his desk or maybe dinner is delayed tonight. The wise father will first seek understanding of Mom's day before passing judgment

on what he sees. All the more reason when you get home, make sure those first words spoken are uplifting, not condemning. They should be words that speak life and build up, not words that tear down or wound.

What then is a husband's reasonable duty towards his wife?

He is to stand behind his wife as a <u>support</u> to her

He is to stand next to his wife as a <u>friend</u> to her

He is to stand in front of his wife as a <u>protector</u> of her

A husband is to live with his wife in understanding, honoring her in both as a wife and as a mother.

Visit One

Chapter One Summary
Transitions

1. The period between 12 and 18 months is a bridge linking babyhood with toddlerhood.

2. Feeding, wake and naptime continue as the three activities of your pretoddler's day.

3. Feeding transitions include:

   a. nursing/formula to whole milk

   b. bottle to sippy cup

   c. baby foods to family meals

   d. highchair to booster seat

   e. separate mealtimes to family mealtimes

4. Nap transitions: two to one nap by 18 months of age.

5. Less naptime creates more waketime activities for baby and Mom

6. Pretoddlers are too young to be reasoned with — too mobile to be left alone.

Chapter Two Summary
Parenting Goals

1. Learn to manage your baby's behavioral 'assets'.

2. Avoid creating any new behavioral 'liabilities'.

3. Your primary goal for the next six months is not to lose any ground; by not losing any ground, you are gaining ground.

4. The word "unpredictable" describes what any day may look like with a pretoddler.

5. "Persevere" when things do not go according to plan, stay mindful of your parenting goals.

6. "Concrete" examples help pretoddlers learn.

7. Remember our guiding principle: Begin as you mean to go.

Chapter Three Summary
Words to Fathers

1. *Appreciation*: One of the greatest gifts a husband can give his wife are words that encourage.

2. *Empathy*: A husband's willingness to fully understand the activities of a mother's day.

3. *Like Minded*: Having a mutually agreed upon direction for parenting.

4. *Accountability*: A willingness to have your decisions and judgments questioned by your spouse.

5. *Knowing "Why"*: Asking questions to become fully engaged in parenting.

6. *Mutual Commitment*: a well informed husband helps make for a better Dad.

7. *Understanding*: The wise father will first seek understanding from Mom before passing judgment on what he sees when he walks through the door.

8. *Speak Life*: Using words that build up and encourage rather than discourage or dishearten.

Visit One — Questions for Review

1. Name at least five transitions, (exchanges) that will take place between twelve and eighteen months.

   a.

   b.

   c.

   d.
   e.

2. What does the word "amusement" mean and what is the warning concerning playtime?

3. According to the authors "the primary goal for pretoddler parenting is not to focus on gaining ground, but rather focus more on not losing any ground." What does that mean to you as a parent?

4. Name some behavioral assets worth managing and protecting.

5. What does the following statement imply? "Go into this pretoddler phase with full expectation that "unpredictable" will become a way of life for the next six months."

6. According to the authors, what is one of the greatest gifts parents can give to their children? Explain your answer.

7. Dad, what does it mean to "seek understanding" when you arrive home at night?

Visit Two

Food and Naptime Transitions

Chapter Four

Mealtime Basics

The primary cottage industry of a pretoddler is play and exploration of his expanding universe. His interests are greatly enhanced once he achieves walking. He is filled with energy. His curiosity will not allow him to just sit still or do nothing. He is constantly on the go, moving, exploring, rearranging and touching everything. Mom says "Sit still", his body says "Wiggle."

If a child possessed the wisdom and reason to govern healthy food, sleep and waketime choices, then by all means let the child lead. But it is precisely because he lacks these qualities that the theme: "Mother knows best" should continue to reign supreme, especially when it comes to the three activities of your pretoddler's day: mealtime, waketime and naptime. In one sense, the task of maintaining good mealtime and sleep routines are the most important activities in your pretoddler's day, even more important than waketime activities. That is in part because how a pretoddler behaves during the time he is awake often depends on how well-rested and well-fed he is.

Actually maintaining healthy mealtime and nap regiments are two of the easier aspects of pretoddler training. This definitive pronouncement can be interpreted one of two ways. It could mean there is less challenge with these activities then with waketime, or it could mean, waketime is so challenging that mealtime and sleep management look easy. Regardless of how you interpret our statement, we'll take up mealtime and naptime transitions in this visit and the slightly more challenging waketime activities in Visits Three and Four.

Where are We Going?

The topics below not only represent the most commonly asked questions relating to food transitions, but also represent a body of knowledge relevant to your child's good nutrition. We divided our discussion of mealtime into three general categories. They include:

- Liquid Transitions
- Solid Foods
- Food challenges

As we work through our mealtime recommendations, please stay mindful that the term "pretoddler" refers specifically to the ages between twelve and eighteen months.

THE WHOLE MILK TRANSITION

Most pediatricians recommend parents start their children on whole, (cow's) milk around their first birthday, not before. A baby's digestive system is not able to sufficiently breakdown and process dairy products. But after the first birthday, everything changes when it comes to whole milk. Whole milk is a great source of calcium, phosphorus, Vitamin A, and magnesium. It comes fortified with Vitamin D. This vitamin in particular helps the body absorb the calcium it needs. Along with its protein properties, whole milk is necessary for building strong bones and teeth and is a great source of carbohydrates which fuel a pretoddler's daily energy needs. Milk has been shown to help the body regulate blood coagulation and muscle control. There is some theoretical evidence suggesting that when a pretoddler receives sufficient calcium in his early years, that he'll have a lower risk of high blood pressure, strokes, colon cancer, and hip fractures later in life. Whole milk does have one downside, that being a limited source of iron. A child should be receiving his daily requirement for iron from other table foods. (More on this point later)

HOW MUCH AND WHEN?

Between twelve and twenty-four months milk should be viewed as a complement to each meal and not as a meal itself as it was during infancy. How many ounces of whole milk should a pretoddler receive in a 24-hour period? Your pretoddler's milk intake should average twenty-four ounces in a 24-hour period. Spread equally between breakfast, lunch, afternoon snack and dinner, a mother can offer four, 6 ounce servings in a sippy cup or three, 8 ounce servings at each main meal and offer water or diluted juice at snack-time.

Whole Milk and Iron Deficiency

Be careful with the amount of milk you put in the sippy cup. Most sippy cups hold eight ounces, so make sure you are not unintentionally offering, four, eight-ounce servings per day. That brings us back to the concern over iron deficiency in your baby's diet.

For clarity sake please understand that there are no negative properties within whole milk that causes iron deficiency within young children. The warning concerning too much milk is related to the *satiating* influence of milk. Milk fills up little tummies very quickly. Full tummies do not eat sufficient amounts of other table foods that provide the necessary iron needed.

Why is this a big deal? Because iron is important to growth and necessary for brain development and learning. It is a necessary requirement to make red blood cells which transport oxygen through the body. Also, diminished iron supply can cause anemia. A good alternative source of iron is fortified cereal and is something Mom can continue to offer for the next six to twelve months. Other sources include: poultry, fish, meats, enriched grains and even tofu. (Yuck!)

2% and Non-Fat Milk

Health conscious mothers might assume that 2% (or non-fat) milk would be a healthier alternative to whole milk. Actually it is just the opposite for pretoddlers. Low fat and non-fat milk lack the nutritional properties necessary for brain and central nervous system development — that being 'fats'. It is only after the second year that parents can begin to offer 2% or non-fat milk.

BOTTLE TO SIPPY CUP TRANSITION

The American Academy of Pediatrics cites a child's first birthday as the appropriate time to move from bottle to sippy cup exclusively. There are two reasons for this. First, pretoddlers are developmentally ready to make the switch. They are at an age in which they can control a greater flow of milk into their mouth compared to the constricted flow that comes by way of the bottle. Second, parents tend to offer more milk when using a bottle, especially during this critical transition time when less milk is required.

While his first birthday is an ideal age to make the transition, some Moms might extend it a month or two longer. Unless there is a medical reason for this, we suggest you work to wean your child completely soon after his first birthday. Suggestions on how to make this a smooth transition are offered below.

Sippy Cup Options

Take a stroll down the baby aisle of your local supermarket and discover the world of sippy cups. They come in all styles, colors, sizes and most have spill-free lids and are easy for little hands to hold. A sippy cup with a straw feature provides some advantages. First, because there is limited tilting action, pretoddlers are less prone to drool their milk with a straw compared to a regular cup. Second, once the child has mastered the straw feature, any straw in any cup will do. This works to Mom's advantage when she is out or when the sippy cup is not handy or available. Of course, using a plain plastic cup, like the one you had when you were a toddler will also work just fine.

TWO CHALLENGES

While pretoddlers have no inherent need for a bottle after twelve months some kids just get overly attached to it. While it may not happen in all homes, there are two common challenges linked to this transition:

1. The child who loves his bottle

2. The child adjusting to the taste of whole milk

The Child Who Loves His Bottle

As stated above, it's at one year of age that children should take their liquid feedings exclusively from a sippy cup. That means the bottle is not necessary and the sooner your pretod-dler can part with it, the better. We all know that a bottle can become an unwelcome *transitional object* as a baby moves into his second year of life. Transitional objects are items that a child becomes comfortable with or dependent on. Some will be car-ried into the toddler years, such as a favorite blanket, teddy bear or stuffed animal. No problem with these items. But there are some transitional objects that parents my need to take the lead on in order to make a successful separation. The bottle is one of these.

Unfortunately, the bottle-to-cup transition is not always as easy as it sounds because like all of us, once we get used to something familiar it is hard to give it up. Fortunately, this is one of the easier pretoddler challenges to remedy. If you haven't already, start by exchanging the sippy cup for the bottle at one mealtime. Lunchtime is probably the easiest to start with, but whatever meal you decide, stay with it. Over the next several days gradually work towards eliminating the bottle from other meals, one meal at a time. Before you know it, the bottle will be gone and your child will be content with his nifty little sippy cup.

Adjusting to the Taste of Whole Milk

For some children, the switch from formula or breast milk to whole milk will only take a day or so. For others, it will be a gradual transition over the course of a couple of weeks. For some children getting used to the taste of whole milk is the big challenge. The best way to facilitate this transition is by mixing the whole milk with formula (or expressed breast milk) and over several days, gradually adding less formula or breast milk until you reach 100% cow's milk. Accepting the difference in taste is also aided when the child is actually thirsty. If this is an issue with your child, consider offering milk toward the end of the meal. Satisfying thirst becomes the motivator to drink. This is not a big hurdle to overcome when done early. The longer you wait the more difficult it will be.

BREAST MILK TO COW'S MILK

The American Academy of Pediatrics recommends breast milk as the ideal food for the first year of life. After a year however, the nutritional benefits of breast milk cannot keep up with the daily requirements of an active pretoddler and whole milk is a necessary alternative to meet the growing demands on your child's body and mind. No problem if you choose to continue breast feeding beyond a year, but please stay mindful that your baby needs the calories derived from table food and whole milk. Breast milk is no longer a sufficient source of nutrition by itself.

JUICES AND WATER

Juices and water are usually introduced to infants around eight months of age. But where do they fit into your pretoddler's diet, if at all? Actually, juices can be used more as a treat than a snack drink. By this we mean, during the pretoddler and early toddlers months, offering juices (diluted with water by 50%) might only be a once or twice a week occurrence. That is because fruit juices are not necessary if you are offering adequate fruits during mealtimes. In fact, fruit juices are not an acceptable substitute for fresh fruits, nor are they a healthy substitute for milk. Too many juices suppress hunger which keeps kids away from other nutritional foods required for growth.

For the tidy-minded mom, the "where" of fruit juices is equally important. We recommend limiting any juice treat to a highchair or booster seat. Mom has enough to do without cleaning up spills that occur when a pretoddler is free-ranging the living room with a liquid in hand. Remember the battle cry: *Begin as you mean to go.*

You might wonder if water is necessary if your child is getting plenty of liquids from milk and juices. The short answer is "Absolutely!" Keep water available and offer a drink periodically, even if it is only a sip. Do this especially during the hot summer months and the confined winter months when heaters are in constant use. As your pretoddler is able to manage some freedoms you may consider leaving a cup in a child-friendly location that is easily accessible to him. Of course, the 'no-wandering in the house' rule still applies.

WHAT IS LACTOSE INTOLERANCE?

If you give your child a cup of milk and it produces diarrhea every time, this signals a dietary problem, possibly a condition known as *lactose intolerance*. This is a condition of the body, not a disease. Digestively speaking, lactose intolerance is the inability of the small intestine to fully digest the lactose (milk sugars) derived from dairy products. This results in abdominal discomfort, including cramping, gas, diarrhea, and nausea.

It is possible that a child may not show any reaction to milk during infancy, but symptoms appear after his first birthday. This is because the ability to produce *lactase*, (the digestive stimulus that actually breaks down the sugars) gradually declines as the child grows older. That is why the onset of symptoms can show up months or even years later. The problem is not associated with birth but with growth. If you start to notice any of the symptoms above after introducing your pretoddler to cow's milk or dairy products, contact his doctor. A test will be performed and once diagnosed, the condition can be easily and successfully managed.

Lactose intolerance is a graded condition, meaning there is a range within the normal treatment protocol. A confirmed diagnosis does not always mean a total abandonment of dairy products. Your pediatrician will direct you on steps to determine what your child can manage. Without milk or dairy products in your pretoddler's diet, getting enough calcium in a twenty-four hour period becomes a challenge. Again, your pediatrician will direct you to healthy calcium substitutes.

If you have a strong family history of lactose intolerance (or food allergies for that matter), the probability of your offspring having this condition is also very high. To get a clear picture of your family medical history, ask questions of your parents, in-laws, aunts, uncles and cousins.

Chapter Five
Babyfood to Table Food

A good place to start this discussion is with terminology. How do you define 'table food'? Table food is any suitable food source that is made at home and is the same food served to the siblings and parents. Most children make the transition from baby food to table food by their first birthday. Once the transition is made, then store bought baby food is no longer necessary, except for the possible exception of iron fortified baby cereal.

When it comes to the table food transition, moms should think in terms of three meals a day; breakfast, lunch, dinner and an afternoon snack. (There may be an occasion in which your child might need a morning snack because of the activities planned for the day.) When it comes to "how" much table food; your pretoddler requires approximately 1,000 calories per day to meet his growth, energy, and nutritional needs. This requirement continues until his second birthday. A 1,000 calories may not seem to you as an adult like a lot of food, but it is plenty of nutrition for a pretoddler.

From the beginning of time and throughout history, mothers have always been concerned with the question of food sufficiency. How do you know if your child is getting enough? There are two ways to monitor adequate calorie intake. First, most pretoddlers will stop eating when their tummy is full. The main concern here is whether he is filling up on liquids rather than appropriate table foods. A second way is to keep track of calories by reading product labeling and serving sizes. After a few weeks, preparing adequate portions with sufficient calories will become second nature to you. Like all of us, a balanced diet is necessary and some familiarity with the food groups is helpful.

Food Groups

Grains: Whole wheat bread and rolls, pasta, English muffins, cereals, oatmeal, brown rice, grits, pancakes, and toast

Meats/Protein: Fish, poultry, beef, pork, eggs and dry beans

Vegetables: Sweet potatoes, squash, pumpkin, beets, cooked carrots, green beans, tomatoes, broccoli, collards, peas, zucchini, kale, and lima beans

Fruits: Apples, applesauce, apricots, bananas, cantaloupe, strawberries, watermelon, tangerines, mangoes, melons, peaches, pineapples, and 100% fruit juice

Dairy: Whole milk, yogurt, cheese, cottage cheese, pudding, custard and ice cream

In reviewing the list above, you will notice the foods are grouped together because they share similar nutritional properties. The list below demonstrates the daily requirements from each group.

Grains: 3 ounces per day
Proteins: 2 ounces per day
Vegetables: 1 cup per day

Fruits: 1 cup per day
Dairy: 20-24 ounces per day from milk (and yogurt, cheese or other calcium rich foods).

HEALTHY FOOD SOURCES

Although the foods above contain all the nutritional benefits your pretoddler needs, the question of vitamin supplements is quit common. Under normal circumstances, if your pretoddler is receiving proper nourishment derived from the basic food groups, vitamin supplements are not necessary. However, in the case of a vegetarian diet, or a diet restricted because of food allergies, check with your health-care provider for the necessary supplements that may be missing as a result of food restrictions.

Combining Foods

There are benefits to combining foods, especially if you have a pretoddler that struggles with fruits and vegetables. To meet this challenge, consider creative alternatives that basically disguises healthy foods in a fun food serving. For example, making "smoothies" using milk, yogurt and fresh fruits. Here's a favorite recipe provided by Paige, one of our assistants.

1 cup milk (whole or skim)
1 cup non-fat vanilla yogurt
1 cup 1-minute oatmeal (mixed with just enough water to make a paste)
Select fresh or frozen fruit of your choice

Mix ingredients in blender, then serve immediately or refrigerate. (Because pretoddlers and toddlers love to use straws you may need to alter either the amount of milk or the amount of oatmeal to reduce the thickness of the drink.)

How about a moist, soft bread packed with goodness. Zucchini bread is a great place to hide those nutritional but maybe not so favorite foods. Get imaginative. Here is another favorite provided by Tara, one of our consulting mothers. (This recipe makes 24 servings):

Ingredients:
½ cup (optional) dried fruit
½ Tbsp baking powder
⅓ cup oil
1 Tbsp baking soda
1 cup shredded carrot
1 cup shredded zucchini
1 to 1½ cup of sugar
2 tsp cinnamon
2 cups vanilla yogurt
3 cups white flour, (or 2 cups white 1 cup whole wheat flower)
3 eggs
3 Tbsp apple sauce
8 tsp wheat gluten (bran)

Preheat oven to 375. Beat eggs until foamy then add sugar, oil, yogurt, applesauce, cinnamon, zucchini, carrot, (and dried fruit-optional). Mix well. In a separate bowl, sift together flour, salt, baking soda, wheat gluten (bran) and baking powder. Add dry ingredients slowly to the yogurt mixture and mix until moist. Pour into 2 greased and floured 9 x 5 x 13-inch loaf pans. Bake for 50-55 min. Loaves should be golden brown on top when coming out of oven.

The Incredible Egg

Eggs are a great source of protein, easy to chew and swallow and can be offered at any meal. (One to five eggs per week is sufficient.) Keep in mind that children between the ages of one and two years do not have the same dietary restrictions as adults or older children, especially when it comes to eggs. Where fats and even cholesterol are restricted for good adult nutrition, these are requirements for a pretoddler's diet. Foods higher in fat and cholesterol actually spur growth and meet their nutritional needs. (When talking about fats, we are not referring to 'junk food' fats.)

Please stay mindful that the general recommendations for one egg per day includes eggs that are eaten as an ingredient of other foods, such as breads or puddings. The American Heart Association calculates that if you use four eggs to bake a cake, and eat between two to eight pieces (depending on size), that is the equivalent of adding another egg to your diet. What is important for your pretoddler is a diet consisting of a wide variety of foods that provide the appropriate balance of nutrients needed.

Eggs come with a secret advantage. Whether scrambled or served as an omelet, they are a mom's secret weapon, her Trojan Horse. Scrambled eggs and omelets can hide the most detestable vegetable known to your child. Add a little cheese and you are back in control of your pretoddler's diet.

ESTABLISHING A PRIMARY MEAL
After their first birthday, the growth rate in pretoddlers slows

down, triggering a corresponding drop in appetite. The one thousand calories needed per day will now come over the course of three meals and an afternoon snack. However, they will not come in four equal servings! At first, it may trouble you that your thirteen-month-old is not eating as much at breakfast and dinner as he does at lunch. This is not unusual, but actually quite normal.

Nutrition is really all about averages, not equal portions. Don't panic if your child seems less hungry today than yesterday, or he is more interested in his carbohydrates than his proteins. Instead, monitor his nutritional habits over a one, two or even three day period. Pretoddlers tend to establish a primary meal, meaning a mealtime where he consistently eats more food each day than at other meals. For example, at lunchtime he ravenously eats everything in sight but barely touches his dinner. This irregularity of food consumption from meal to meal is nothing to be concerned about. Again, this is normal and is part of the transition from babyhood to toddlerhood.

FINGER FOODS
When it comes to finger foods, think healthy and think variety. Finger foods for pretoddlers include cereals, breads, rice, whole wheat pasta, pears, peaches, strawberries, soft cooked squash (cubed, not mashed) or sweet potatoes cooked soft but cubed, bananas and scrambled eggs. To avoid a picky eater, keep presenting a variety of foods, so no one particular taste or texture dominates and pushes other food options out.

Choking Hazards
When offering finger foods, stay mindful of any potential choking hazards. Pretoddlers lack their grinding molars so their

natural inclination is not to chew just swallow. Thus, foods not cut into small pieces pose a choking hazard. To help eliminate this potential, offer finger foods that are soft and small enough to be swallowed if the child does not chew it at all. If you're looking for a good measurement for "bite-size" servings take look at Mom's 'pinky' fingernail, (without acrylic extensions). That's a great measurement.

Foods to avoid at these ages include:

- Raw vegetables
- Raisins
- Dry fruits
- Nuts
- Popcorn
- Grapes (unless cut up)
- Hot dogs
- Hard cheese
- Gum
- Seeds
- Candy

(Check with your pretoddler's pediatrician for more items that can be added to this list.) One last word of caution; never leave your pretoddler unattended during mealtime, especially with a non-responsible sibling. Many reported incidents of choking happen as a result of an overly assertive sibling offering the wrong food to little brother. A four-year-old should not be the dietary supervisor of his fifteen-month-old sibling.

FROM FINGER FOODS TO UTENSILS
Long before they are able to master its purpose, pretoddlers become fascinated with a spoon (and when appropriate a fork). As a general rule, do not allow your child to continually do something in a wrong way. There is no purpose in allowing a child to hold a utensil he doesn't have the coordination to use properly. But when you begin to see the signs of interest and

ability, consider introducing the spoon.

The process of learning to use a spoon is predictable among children and they all seem to go through the same steps on their way to mastery. By sixteen months of age, your son may hold the spoon in one hand while self feeding with his fingers from the other. This usually transitions to picking food up with his fingers and placing it onto the spoon. From there he attempts to bring it to his mouth but any food that falls off is then retrieved with his fingers. But instead of returning the food to the spoon, he shovels it directly to his mouth. Once the fallen crumb pieces are in the mouth, the entire process starts again.

Eventually, the child's coordination reaches the point that he is able to keep most of the food on his spoon until it gets to his mouth. When that happens, finger feeding is occasional and often only when necessary because of the type of food offered.

Why are we offering such a detailed description? To point out that the finger food/utensil transition will take time, patience and encouragement. While some parents start as early as sixteen months, you might want to wait until eighteen months before earnestly pushing forward with the spoon. Most children sufficiently master the spoon/fork combination between twenty to twenty-four months.

SNACKS AND TREATS

It has been said, "When sweets are out of a toddler's sight they are out of mind." Creating right habits for snacks is a big part of smart nutrition. The best snacks will be low in sugar and salt. Whole-grain breakfast cereals, graham crackers, small pieces of cheese, cut-up fruit or softened vegetables are all wonderful snack options served after the afternoon nap.

One of the first rules relating to snacks is to make sure they do not become a full meal. A snack is a snack. Anytime you find that one of the three mealtimes is affected, recalibrate the amount of snacks offered but at these ages, do not remove them completely. Here are a few helpful hints about snacking:

1. Use in moderation. Do not let snacks detract from a hearty appetite.

2. Do not use food to avoid conflict. It's generally not wise to attempt to influence a child's behavior by offering a snack.

3. Do not use food to pacify sad emotions.

4. Keep the place for snacking consistent, such as a booster seat or highchair.

5. Avoid allowing your child to wander around the house or store with a drink or snack in his hand.

6. As a general suggestion, offer snacks in the afternoon, such as after your child wakes up from his nap.

For purposes of clarification, we consider a treat something different than a snack. Where a snack is a necessary afternoon mini-meal offered with nutrition in mind, a treat is a special pleasure that may happen once or twice a week. It could be a cookie, a few pieces of sugar free popsicles or a fruit drink. Keep the treats to a minimum and keep the snacks healthy.

Chapter Six

Food Challenges

———◦———

There are some mealtime situations that seem to have Mom warring against unknown forces summoned by the will of her child. Although she is an otherwise reasonable woman, she now contemplates the possibility that her child carries way too many genetic influences from his father's side of the family. But wait; there is hope for Mom and child, (and Dad). The application of a little knowledge, understanding and wisdom will help the 'nice lady' gain control over the most trying situations. Let's consider a few pretoddler mealtime challenges.

THE PICKY EATER

It all sounds so simple. A child is hungry, he eats and the stomach takes over from there. Yet, ask any experienced Mom of a pretoddler and you discover there are behaviors associated with mealtimes that are not so simple. Take the picky eater for example. Is this challenge the product of birth or parenting? Excluding a medical condition, picky eaters are created, not born. Where do you begin to figure this one out?

As a parent, evaluate your own relationship to food. Are you overly concerned with nutritional intake? Are you a picky eater? Perhaps you are a junk food connoisseur. As hard as it may be, try not to pass on any of your extreme preoccupations with food. Family mealtime and the kitchen table should not become a war zone. Try to make meals a pleasant experience for everyone sharing the meal.

Like all of us, pretoddlers can and will show preferences in taste. But don't rush into the belief or the phrase: "Oh, he doesn't like it," then offer something else. While yes, you will work to serve your child enjoyable foods, you must also consider what food traditions complements the need and desires of the entire family. When age-appropriate, offer your child the same foods your family normally eats while keeping in mind that what a pretoddler refuses to eat today may become his favorite food tomorrow! Here is the good news: The "spirit of the picky eater" can by pass your house when you apply a few common-sense principles.

Consider Serving Size: Start with small portions and let the child request more food. A small portion for a pretoddler can range between a teaspoon to a tablespoon serving.

Keep a Feeding Schedule: Have regular times scheduled for meals and stick to them as often as possible. This will help maintain your child's hunger mechanism.

Avoid Excessive Drinks: Are you giving your child too many fruit drinks? An appropriate snack amount is 6 ounces. Pushing liquid snacks too close to dinner time can decrease a child's appetite to the point that he is not sufficiently hungry at dinner to eat foods that are not 'favorites'.

Monitor the Snacks: A child that eats too little and just picks at meals is a child who is probably snacking too much during the day. He is never hungry enough to eat full meals.

Appetite versus Hunger

We have all experienced it. Even now as I write this paragraph my mind drifts to a pleasant memory of last night's dinner. There is a big slice of pizza left over with a brown-bubbled crust spot. I admit, I'm not really hungry but my memory tells me it is something that I would enjoy — right now, even though I just had breakfast an hour ago. So how is it that our tummy says "no" to food, but our pleasure senses scream "bring it on"? That's what appetite does. Appetite does not respond to need but to want. It's a pleasure sensation, triggered by the sight, smell and memory of food.

In parenting, we tend to interchange the words, hunger and appetite as if they mean the same thing. They don't and in fact, they are completely different biological processes. Hunger is a physical sensation, a response triggered by a drop in blood sugar, which in turn sends a message to the brain calling for more food. Appetite is external and driven by desire, regardless of actual need.

How does this apply to pretoddlers and mealtime? If you're the type of mother concerned that your child will not get enough food there is a tendency to allow the child's appetite to control what you serve rather than actual hunger. You place scramble eggs in front of your fifteen month old, who rejects them outright, (although they were fine yesterday). Next you ask, "Would you like toast instead?" "Okay, how about toast with a little jam on it?" Wait, who is in control here? Mom or the child's appetite? There will always be a time for fun foods, but when they are served to the point where a child refuses to eat anything else, well, Mom has created a mealtime monster, the unpredictable spirit of the "picky eater".

Appetite and the Picky Eater

This happens when the actual biological mechanism of hunger is suppressed because the child has too many "appetizing" treats throughout the day, or because he has learned that if he waits long enough, "Mom will give me something better". Appetite is not the silent partner of hunger rather it is often the enemy. Learn to monitor real need, keep your mealtime routine going, limit the number of treats and stay mindful that just because your little one shows a preference for one food, it doesn't mean abandoning other foods you deem appropriate.

SUDDEN REFUSAL OF FAVORITE FOODS

What should a parent do when their child suddenly refuses to eat a food that up to yesterday was his favorite? Our first response is to tell you not to worry about it because this is not uncommon during the pretoddler phase. Children do not view food the way adults do. A favorite food is something they might delight in every day for two weeks while an adult can easily tire if the same food is served two days in a row. If the "all of a sudden" distaste happens with your little one, examine whether the challenge is a:

1. <u>Nutrition Issue</u>: The child needs the food because it is important to his diet

2. <u>Submission Issue</u>: The child is saying "No" to Mom and not the food

3. <u>Appetite Issue</u>: The child is hooked on preference

4. <u>Mommy Issue</u>: "I'm the mother and you will learn to like this food!"

If the primary concern is nutrition, camouflage the food in

other foods. Hide those formally favorite green beans in an egg, or mix them in Tara's low-fat Zucchini bread. If submission is the issue, this will show up in other areas throughout the day. Work on "Mommy knows best" in those moments of challenge, rather than making food the issue. If it's an appetite issue, revisit the types of treats your offer. If it is a "Mommy" issue, then learn balance by offering small samples of food without insisting the child eat everything. Be patient, one day your child will enjoy the same foods the family enjoys.

What if you know your pretoddler likes a particular food but stubbornly refuses to eat it? What if it is a submission issue? Without getting too far ahead of our teaching in Visit Four, (Mealtime Behavior and Correction), we would like to introduce a true life scenario that has a happy ending. Seventeen-month-old Jenna went on a fruit strike. She knew if she waited long enough or fussed hard enough Mom would give her some fun tasting carbohydrates. Mom had other plans.

Realizing a pattern was developing and knowing bananas were a favorite food, Mom served Jenna a small portion, and then applied her motherly resolve. Jenna's highchair was moved to a boring spot in the kitchen and the battle of the wills began. An hour and-a-half later, Jenna surrendered to Mom and the bananas were gone. (Yes, there was some fussing but it was matched by motherly wisdom and resolve.)

End of story? Not yet. The next morning, (after a good nights rest) Mom placed a serving of bananas on Jenna's highchair tray. She then brought Jenna to her meal. We wish we could report all went perfect, but Jenna went on strike again but only for forty-five minutes this time. Suddenly, the bananas were gone and Jenna was happy.

The next day, Mom offered a few grapes with the bananas.

We are pleased to report the fruit-hunger strike was over in ten seconds. Since that episode, our dear Jenna eats whatever Mom places in front of her.

For Jenna's Mom, this was a combination of three issues, *nutrition, submission* and *appetite*. All three became players in the scenario, but all three were conquered with Mom's resolve in keeping Jenna in the highchair until her meal was done. Will this strategy work for all children all the time? We don't know. But without resolve or clear nutritional goals, food challenges will begin to grow in number and complexity.

TABLE FOODS AND DIGESTIVE CHALLENGES

Given the change in a pretoddler's diet from baby food to table food, there may come a time when stool softeners might be necessary if constipation becomes a problem. Constipation, whether in adults or children, is usually associated with the result of insufficient liquid intake combined with a diet too high in dairy products, such as milk and cheese, or foods such as bananas, cooked carrots and processed meats.

While the problem is best treated with a change in diet, there are a number of over-the-counter stool softeners. Before heading off to the local pharmacy, first try changing your child's diet. Home remedies include increasing a daily regiment of fruits and vegetables, fiber-filled foods and bran such as whole wheat bread, bran muffins and cereals. Of course the most important item is an increase in liquids. Keep a sippy cup of water handy and continue to offer it throughout the day.

If the problem persists, notify your child's doctor. He or she may prescribe a particular stool softener. These are usually over-the-counter products that are safe and effective. Stool softeners however, should not be confused with laxatives. Laxatives in a pretoddler's body can be dangerous if given without medical supervision or direction.

CUTTING TEETH AND HUNGER

Cutting teeth does affect hunger in pretoddlers because pain has a way of suppressing the hunger drive. Teething during baby-hood is actually less painful than during the pretoddler months. This is due to the location and type of teeth. The eight front incisors (used for biting rather than chewing), usually appear around six months of age. Incisors cut through the gums fairly easily. Although they cause swelling and drooling, they are not as painful as cutting molars. Unlike the little thin, flat teeth dropping out of the front of the mouth, molars are big square blocks, (relatively speaking) breaking through the gums in the back of the mouth. These teeth are used for chewing. The first set of molars appear between twelve and fifteen months, fol-lowed ten months later by the second set.

Unfortunately, the process of erruption can extend five to seven days, accompanied by pain, irritability, low-grade fever and loss of appetite. Before the erruption of teeth, the body tends to store enough fats and nutritional reserves, so one week of eating less is usually not a health concern. During this time, do not worry as much about your feeding routine. Remember context rules. Offer nutritious snacks and fluids, (milk, juice and water) throughout the day. A teething pretoddler enjoys chewing on chilled food sources such as frozen waffles or bananas. You can visit the Internet to read about "teething feed-ers". These are used to safely offer chilled or frozen vegetables during teething, reducing the risk of choking.

Your friend comments on your child's irritability and states "He's probably cutting his molars." The greatest medical danger associated with cutting teeth is wrongly assuming that your pretoddler's mild fever and irritability is related to them. While there may be a high probability your friend is correct, don't put one hundred percent confidence in that assessment. If the low-grade fever or loss of appetite is accompanied by your child pulling on his ear, vomiting or diarrhea, be sure to contact his doctor. These are not all teething symptoms although they may appear at the same time. Before you offer any medication, including baby aspirin or Tylenol, contact your child's pediatrician.

SIGNING SKILLS - 'NEVER TOO LATE'

The urgent email asked, "My son throws his food off the high-chair to signal he is done eating. What should I do?" Children will clear food from their tray, but at these ages it is not done out of a heart bent on mischievousness or helpfulness, but the inability to communicate. Obviously, clearing his serving tray by dropping food on the floor is his way of saying, "All done". But signing "All done" is a much better alternative. If you haven't introduced sign language to your pretoddler, this is a good time to start.

It is never too late to take advantage of a second language. Although the sign, "All done" is your immediate need, we still recommend starting with the "Please" sign and then move to "Thank you", followed by "All done". We start with the "Please" sign because it is the only one that represents an act of submission. With the "please" sign, your child learns how to seek what he needs by asking rather than telling you. This pays big dividends in the future when the toddlerhood battles of the wills begin to turn a young mom's hair gray.

If just beginning with sign language, be patient. Teaching

the fundamentals of signing will take some time but be consistent and persevere. Your pretoddler will not only catch up quickly but find this form of communication satisfies his needs and yours. In time signing will become his second language and yours.

Please
(Place right hand over heart and pull back toward right arm)

Thank You:
(Place tips of the hand (fingers together) against the mouth and throw hand forward, similar to blowing a kiss.)

Once your child has a working understanding of these basic languages, but refuses to sign, use natural consequences to reinforce the correct response. For example, if he wants a toy, but refuses to sign "please", withhold the toy. If it is a cookie, withhold the cookie.

<u>*All Done*</u>:

Put hands in front of you with fingers spread apart. Turn hands back and forth.

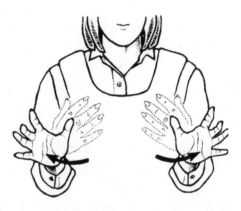

However, try not to get into a power struggle over food at mealtimes. You should not withhold primary meals because your baby doesn't sign. In the context of mealtime you might take his little hand and sign please with him, saying to him, "let's do please" then give him his food. You will have plenty of opportunity to work on sign language during the day other than mealtimes. Take advantage of those opportunities. Here are some virtuous reasons to teach basic sign language to your pretoddler.

• Through signing you are teaching and reinforcing habits of self-control.

- Signing eliminates wrong communication methods by providing right modes of expression.

- Signing aids discretionary correction in the future. There will be times when you cannot easily correct your child publicly or verbally. The silence of signing, together with Mom's facial expression, communicates the same intent as verbal correction.

- You are actually teaching your child a second language during a time in the child's life when he or she is most receptive to language formation.

THE BOOSTER SEAT

Your pretoddler is getting too big for the highchair but still too small to reach the top of a table from a chair. This is when a booster seat comes into play. The principle function of a booster seat is found in its name – it gives pretoddlers just the right boost they need.

What do parents need to know about this plastic piece of molded furniture? Safety is the first concern. A good booster seat has two straps, one to fasten the booster seat to the chair and a second one that secures the child to the booster seat. Apart from that, making the transition from highchair to booster seat comes toward the end of the pretoddler phase, around eighteen months of age. Mom and Dad decide when the child makes this transition – not the child!

Parents will inquire as to whether a booster seat is absolutely necessary. No, it is not. However, if a child is kneeling on an adult-size chair, he usually lacks the coordination to move food from plate to mouth without creating an enormous mess. A booster seat helps reduce the mess.

THE IMPORTANCE OF FAMILY MEALTIME

A mother will ask, "Should we work on keeping our pretoddler at the family meal even though he has already eaten?" Yes, by all means! This is a good habit even if it means you offer some bite-size cereal or bring a toy to the highchair. It is all about the moment and mealtime is all about moments that build memories.

When you add up all the hours a typical family spends at mealtime over the years a child lives in the home, you come to realize this is one of the greatest opportunities to lead, teach, and encourage your children. At mealtime parents model how to serve, listen and speak to others. These are training opportunities that you cannot afford to miss. Children should look forward to mealtimes, not simply because Mom cooked a great meal or to fill their tummies, but because it is the time of day when you come together as a family.

We believe this to be one of the most important attitudes parents should cultivate in the hearts of their children. Mealtime is simultaneously about the present and the future. When your children are grown they will carry with them many family memories. Your children will not remember all the conversations that took place over the years but they will carry with them the strong impression of your family's togetherness. Give them the gift of a beautiful memory and the confidence that no matter what the day has been like, good or bad, there is one moment of each day to looked forward to and that is the mealtime you share together. In this day and age, this is a treasure parents can give their children that can never be taken away and it is free.

DADS AND MEALTIME

There are not many influences more powerful in the life of

children than a father's presence in the home. A father who parents with care and attentiveness gives his children a healthy, stable sense of confidence. Conversely, a father who misses these opportunities reduces his influence and effectiveness as a mentor, leader, guide and friend.

That is why the family mealtime should be a high priority for every father and should not be viewed as just another event of the day. One thing we learned along the way is whether Mom cooked a gourmet meal or ordered food from a favorite take-out, what children really need at a mealtime is availability to Dad! This is the time to silence the phone and turn off the television.

The dinner table has always been the social center of families. This is where children learn to talk, share their feelings, hopes and dreams. Mealtime provides opportunities to catch up on everyone's day. It is at the dinner table that we as families talk, laugh and learn, share our personal successes, and sometimes carry each other's burdens, no matter how small or large. As a Dad, purpose that one day your children will look back with fondness and a sense of family connectedness from all those dinners around the kitchen table and realize this could not happen without Dad's full commitment to the family.

Chapter Seven
Naps and Nighttime Sleep

❧

S leep is an important part of a child's life and will continue to be a vital aspect of your pretoddler's day and night. Naps are not an option based on your child's desires. When naptime comes, your pretoddler must go down. It's that simple. For optimal development, children need their nap.

A pretoddler's ability to take a nap depends to a large extent on the habits the child has developed in his or her first year. As a general rule, your child transitioned to two naps a day at eight months, and continues this pattern into the pretoddler phase. One or both naps may gradually decrease in length of time from two hours to one-and-a half hours and sometimes to one hour. This may happen anytime between fourteen and eighteen months, although the longer your child takes two naps, the better for child and Mom. When transitioning to a single nap, guide your pretoddler to dropping the morning nap and not the afternoon nap. Consider afternoon naps 'sacred sleep'. Here are some questions to consider when working through the nap transitions.

- Are the nap cycles becoming shorter in duration?

- Is your pretoddler becoming inconsistent with his nap routine? For example, are you finding two or three mornings a week he is playing quietly in his crib rather than sleeping?

Is he only sleeping thirty to forty-minutes?

- What is his disposition when waking after taking a shorter nap? If he is consistently fussy and stays that way, then he is not ready to drop the nap.

- Are his nutritional needs being met, both through solids and liquid feedings?

- Is he still sleeping ten to twelve hours at night?

By seventeen months of age, you might begin introducing your pretoddler to one nap a day by skipping the morning nap and beginning the afternoon nap right after lunchtime. You may choose to move lunch up one-half hour for the first couple weeks, evaluating his progress. Never be afraid to go back if necessary to his two-nap a day routine.

Below are two sample schedules that make allowances for nap adjustments. We provided a range of overlapping times because we realize every child and family situation is different. Keep in mind these are only samples and not necessarily how your child's daily routine will look. Be flexible with these times and make adjustments according to what is best for your child and family.

Two Naps a Day

Range of Times	Activity
7:00 - 7:30 am	Wake/eat/playtime
9:00 - 9:30 am	Naptime begins
11:00 -11:30 am	Nap ends
12:00 -12:30 pm	Lunch time
12:30 - 1:30 pm	Playtime
1:00 - 1:30 pm	Naptime begins

3:30 - 4:00 pm	Nap ends/Snack
5:30 - 6:00 pm	Dinner
6:00 - 7:30 pm	Family Time
7:00 - 7:30 pm	To Bed

One Afternoon Nap

Range of Times	Activity
7:00 - 7:30 am	Wake/eat/playtime
7:30 - 9.00 am	Playtime
9:00 - 9:30 am	Light Snack/Juice
9:30 - 11:30 am	Waketime
11:30 - 12:30 pm	Lunch time
12:30 - 1:00 pm	Nap begins
3:00 - 4:00 pm	Nap Ends/Snack
4:00 - 5:30 pm	Waketime
5:30 - 6:00 pm	Dinner
6:00 - 7:30 pm	Family Time
7:00 - 7:30 pm	To Bed

IT'S NAPTIME BUT YOUR CHILD DOESN'T SLEEP

Off and on for two weeks Mom finds her sixteen-month old playing quietly in his crib instead of napping. What is this a sign of, and what should she do? When it comes to nap transitions every child is different and the duration of the transition can range from a week to a month. Learning how to manage the 'two naps to one nap' requires a mother to look for trends in two areas. The first is behavioral. Look for this correlation: If a child is not napping well or not at all during the morning routine, but is showing signs of fatigue before you get to the lunch hour (crankiness, rubbing eyes, or crying), he is probably not ready to drop his morning nap, even if he is playing quietly in his crib.

Looking toward a positive behavioral correlation; if your child is able to sustain a reasonable measure of alertness over a two or three day period and is able to make it to lunchtime without a behavioral meltdown, that is a strong indicator that he is ready to drop his morning nap, or at least he is close to doing so. In some cases, the transition might require a short thirty minute catnap for a couple of weeks or he might need a morning nap every third or forth day. Both of the scenarios described above are effective during this transition.

The second trend looks at the sleep patterns over a twenty-four hour period. Do the math. Dropping a two-hour morning nap is offset by an hour or more increase to the afternoon nap. Net loss? About an hour in a twenty-four hour period. If you find your child is sleeping longer than three hours in the afternoon, then possibly a morning catnap is still necessary.

UNDERSTANDING THE FATIGUE FACTOR

A frustrated Mom asks, "My perfect twelve-month-old sleeper is fighting his naps to the point of fatigue. He is so over-tired that he can't sleep. Should I just let him cry it out?" The correct answer depends on whether this question is about a 'tired' child or a 'fatigued' child. The fatigued child is a uniquely different challenge than the tired one.

Although this was addressed in the *Babywise II* series, a short review here will be helpful since it has implications during the pretoddler phase. The character traits of fatigue are not the same as those of a tired child. The tired child can usually recoup the sleep needed in one 'good' nap or at least with a single twenty-four hour cycle. The fatigued pretoddler is cranky, whiny and nothing can soothe him. The fatigued pretoddler actually has a disruption in the sleep cycles that requires special attention.

If you try to keep your pretoddler up (thinking he will sleep better at the next naptime if he is exhausted), the problem will only get worse. If you attempt to force sleep on the child by not responding to his cries (legitimately born out of fatigue), Mom and Dad can quickly become emotional wrecks and your child will not be helped. Let's look into the context and uniqueness of this challenge.

Healthy sleep has two primary components that most moms are unwilling to give up. The child who sleeps through his naps without waking is one and the child who sleeps in his crib for those naps is the other. While both are important, one may be temporarily suspended for the greater good of the child. By 'greater good' we mean the restoration of his natural sleep rhythms is more important than where he is napping today. How is this accomplished?

Fatigue in children is not much different than fatigue in adults. We all know what it feels like to be so tired that you can't sleep. That's because fatigue attacks the sleep rhythms, preventing a child from entering the ebb and flow of active and relaxed sleep states. It may come as a result of your child's routine being out-of-whack for several days, especially during the time of day when naps are a normal part of his routine. The priority is for Mom to find a non-stressful solution to re-establishing the circadian rhythm.

If the nap challenge is fatigue, find a comfortable chair, a good book, sit down and allow her pretoddler to take his nap in your arms. When asleep try placing him in his crib. This might extend through a few nap cycles. If he wakes, then just keep him in your arms. When your child begins to show signs during waketme of being well rested, back to the crib we go. Does this work? Yes, most definitely. It works because the tension between the need for sleep and the place for sleep is temporarily suspended while your pretoddler is receiving restorative sleep. Yet, you are not creating a sleep prop because this sleep adjustment is for a few nap cycles while you are satisfying his real sleep need by helping him overcome the fatigue.

Prevention is, of course, the best medicine. It always is, and will always be. Try to think through how your good sleeper became a fatigued child. It didn't just happen, and one day's suspension of your pretoddler's routine will not foster this condition. Two or three days of continual disruption may. Take a look at what is going on in your home and with his schedule and make the appropriate adjustments. Do not take this sleep challenge lightly. Optimal alertness comes from optimal sleep. It is during the time of optimal alertness that your child's brain is learning and growing. Poor sleep habits negatively impact the neuro-chemical transmitters that stimulate growth. Manage your pretoddler's sleep assets and minimize his sleep liabilities.

QUESTIONS AND ANSWERS ABOUT NAPS

When it comes to pretoddlers, there are few disruptions that can turn a great nap taker into a challenging child. Fortunately, most challenges have an explanation and can be quickly brought under control. Here are some things to watch out for.

Question One: My baby, who is now thirteen-months-old and has done well with his nap routine until very recently. I'm not sure if I'm doing something wrong or if he's getting ready to drop a nap, but he is waking early from his morning nap. It might be important to know that I also work from home and really need him to take his morning nap. What can I do to facilitate this?

Answer: As mentioned in Visit One, every family and child is different and each family has unique needs calling for unique strategies. Working from home certainly qualifies as one. In the case of a thirteen-month-old, it is too early to drop down to one nap a day. The solution here starts with trying to find out why the child is waking early before attempting to introduce a new nap strategy. If you find yourself in this situation, consider some of these factors.

Waking early might be a signal that he is not eating enough at breakfast. Check his solid and liquid intake. Has there been a change in the general environment? Is a new home going up in the neighborhood, or new construction nearby? Has there been a change in your morning routine?

After making a brief assessment, consider your options. You can try to extend his waketime by thirty to forty-five minutes. Re-adjust his playpen time so it starts when you need to be working. In this context you might offer a small morning juice snack, which will provide enough energy to extend his wake-time a little longer. Just keep in mind, once you begin to adjust the morning nap, that will have an impact on the afternoon nap and possibly bedtime.

Question Two: My child took excellent naps until he hit his one-year-old birthday. Now all of a sudden his naps are very short, waking at forty-five minutes and not going back to sleep.

Answer: It appears there may be two separate issues going on here. The first is waking after forty-five minutes and not falling back to sleep again. At this age, the 'forty-five minute intruder' highlighted in the *On Becoming Babywise* book is not suspect. However the challenge might be the need to fully transition to table foods. Your little one might be hungry and is in need of more calories. Try increasing the amount of solids and make sure you have switched over to whole milk. You might also consider adding a small snack between breakfast and the morning nap if necessary.

The second issue is tied to nap management. First, look at the entire amount of sleep in a twenty-four hour period. Sleeping longer than twelve hours at night might be the culprit here. Consider reducing the nighttime to eleven or twelve hours. That will affect either the bedtime or the morning waketime. Based on which is affected, try to realign his naptimes to correspond with the new bedtime or morning waketime.

At twelve months there is no wiggle room when it comes to naps. Your child needs both. If you find him cranky for days without relief, check his body. Look in his mouth. Are there any signs of his first-year molars? Check for irritation or rash marks, or even a hair twisted around a toe (tourniquet syndrome). Also, please review the section above on pretoddlers and fatigue.

Question Three: My son shows a preference for a long morning nap but fights his afternoon nap. What should I do?

Answer: There are at least two issues here, possibly more. First, remember you are working with a 24-hour sleep strategy. At this age, what are the sleep requirements? He needs ten to twelve hours at night and between three to four hours during the day. Is he getting more or less?

Let's start with reviewing his nighttime sleep. If he is not receiving sufficient sleep at night, it will show up in the morning. Even though he may wake cheerfully, his need for rest will manifest itself very quickly after breakfast. Please note, he is not tired because of the busyness of the morning, but because of the lack of restorative sleep the night before. So the morning nap in this case becomes an extension of his previous nighttime and that is why he is showing a preference for a longer morning nap. However, as a result of a long morning nap, he doesn't sleep as well or as long during the afternoon. If this is the root problem, adjust his bedtime so he is receiving the necessary amount of nighttime sleep.

A second possible contributing factor has a much simpler explanation. Perhaps his morning waketime is too long, so he is going down over tired at his first nap, sleeping longer to compensate. But the corresponding affect is the same as above; he is not sufficiently ready for a good afternoon nap. Less sleep in the afternoon might translate into a cranky pretoddler during dinnertime. If this is the case, manage the morning nap by not letting him sleep as long. That will help him balance out both naptimes. To help further evaluate the challenge, please revisit the sample nap schedules provided in this section.

<u>Question Four</u>: My seventeen-month-old twins are transitioning from two naps to one. But one of the boys is waking early and then waking up his brother who definitely needs more sleep. They share the same room. What can I do?

<u>Answer</u>: If it is possible to separate the boys to different rooms during the two-to-one nap transition, do so. This will enable the boys to receive the appropriate amount of sleep according to their individual sleep needs. As a side note, while it might be tempting to push the twin who needs more sleep to wake-up with his brother to keep them on the same schedule, don't do it. Why? This usually translates into a fussy pretoddler. This

leads to behavioral problems requiring more correction, when all he really needs is more sleep. If there is a silver lining to this challenge, it is knowing this particular sleep challenge is temporary.

Question Five: Our son is eighteen-months-old. Can we transition him from the crib to a youth bed?

Answer: The crib-to-bed transition usually occurs between eighteen and twenty-four months of age and requires training to 'stay in there' when put down. A child who understands what it means to obey, greatly facilitates this transition. Going from a crib to a bed is a freedom. What will keep the child in his bed? Only your word! The goal isn't simply to put your child in a bed, but to have the child stay there all night.

To help make this future transition smooth for you and exciting for your child, include him when going out to purchase any new furniture for his room. Shopping with Mom to pick out his 'big boy' sheets will also motivate him to take ownership of the change. Consider making the transition on the weekend when Dad is home just in case there are some nighttime issues to work through with staying in bed. Dad's presence and encouragement go a long way toward success.

Out of health and safety concerns make sure the bed has side rails. Children move around during sleep more than adults. Side rails are as much for the parents' peace of mind as for the child's safety.

Finally, we recommend that you train our child to ask permission to get out of bed. Common phrases, such as, "Up, please" or "May I get up, please?" are not that difficult for children to learn. Letting your child have verbal access to you is usually enough to keep him from taking a physical freedom of getting out of bed at will.

At this point, you might be reading this and thinking, "no way will he actually stay in bed." Here is some good news for those who are not at this point yet. The crib-to-bed transition is something you will do at the end of the pretoddler phase, not before. That means the months leading up to this time will provide plenty of opportunity to train in necessary compliance. Be aware, the quality of training taking place now will impact how he responds in the future. This is part of our guiding principle, *"begin as you mean to go."* If you mean for him to stay in bed in six months, what do you need to do *now* to facilitate that outcome? In our next visit, we will begin to lay out the foundational strategy that will help you and your child get there.

Visit Two

Chapter One Summary
Mealtime Basics

1. Most pretoddlers can transition to a sippy cup between 12 and 14 months.

2. A pretoddler, on average will receive up to 24 ounces of whole milk per day.

3. Iron deficiency becomes a risk factor when a pretoddler receives more than 24 ounces of milk per day.

4. Pretoddlers should not receive low or non-fat milk before age two.

5. A pretoddler can continue to receive iron-fortified cereal until 18 to 24 months of age.

6. Pretoddlers usually have 3 meals a day with one afternoon snack.

7. Nutritionally speaking, pretoddlers tend to establish a "primary meal" for the day.

8. The spoon and fork can be introduced between 16 and 18 months.

Chapter Two Summary
More Food Transitions

1. For most pretoddlers, pureed baby foods are no longer necessary after 12 months of age.

2. Finger food bite size should be small enough to be easily swallowed even when not chewed properly.

3. Food and drink snacks should be limited to a specific location such as a snack chair or highchair.

4. Picky eaters tend to be the product of training more than genetics.

5. Persevere with your favorite family foods.

6. Become familiar with any family history of food allergies or dietary related medical conditions.

7. Foods that should not be served to pretoddlers include:

   a. raw carrots

   b. nuts

   c. hard candy

   d. popcorn

   e. hot dogs or any skin meats

   f. items with large amounts of processed salt

   g. whole grapes

Chapter Three Summary
Naps and Nighttime Sleep

1. Every child is different when it comes to naps and nap transitions.

2. Naps are still critical during the 12 to 18 month growth phase.

3. Naps transition from two per day gradually to one by 18 months.

4. Learn the difference between a "tired" pretoddler and a "fatigued" pretoddler.

5. Pretoddlers need optimal sleep to achieve optimal alertness required for optimal learning.

6. Persevere with your nap and nighttime sleep training.

7. If your pretoddler is not taking at least one good two-hour nap a day, the problem is with sleep management, not a lack of need.

Visit Two — Questions For Review

1. At what age should whole milk be introduced to your child and how many ounces per day should he be receiving?

2. Is it possible to give a pretoddler too much milk? Explain your answer.

3. What are the dangers associated with offering a pretoddler 2% or non-fat milk?

4. Should a pretoddler receive fortified cereal after his first birthday? Explain your answer.

5. Approximately, how many calories should a pretoddler receive each day?

6. What is a "primary meal"?

7. In the story of Jenna, (the seventeen-month old who went on a fruit strike), what two qualities did her mother possess that brought them successfully through Jenna's food challenge?

8. Learning how to manage the 'two naps to one nap' transition requires a mother to look for trends in two areas. What are they?

Section Three

Boundaries

Chapter Eight
Understanding Boundaries

S everal Middle School students huddled around the inside perimeter of a schoolyard fence. A psychologist from a local university who was passing by subsequently suggested that the fences be taken down. His theory was that the children resented being 'fenced in'. The fences, he concluded, restricted their freedom to roam the playground at will. The fences were taken down. The result? The children began to huddle in the middle of the yard. Why? The children didn't know where the boundaries where. Boundaries give children a sense of security. When the fences came down, their security was stripped away.

HOW CHILDREN LEARN

How far back do theories in early childhood educational stretch? There is a conversation recorded in Jewish history of group of religious leaders responding to a reprimand from one of Israel's prophets. The rebuked leaders asked the prophet, "Does God regard us merely as young children? Are we now to be taught in the same way one teaches a child just weaned?"

This conversation sheds some light on an ancient educational truth, that by all standards, apply today particularly to a pretoddler. And how do you teach young children? According to the account of this conversation, children learn "precept upon precept, and line upon line", *(Isaiah 28:10)*. Amazingly, no truth has as much practical implications for training children today than this single principle from the ancients. Because all learning is progressive ("precept built upon precept"), you cannot move your child into a world of knowledge without first securing a foundation for that knowledge to build on. That is what "precept upon precept" implies.

This idea is reinforced by the repetition of "line upon line." Presented here is the image of a schoolmaster who instructs his pupils by making lines and marks for them to trace and imitate. The complexity of the Hebrew language requires first the learning of strokes before the assembling of a word. Baby steps lead to bigger steps, but baby steps first. Not much has changed in twenty-seven hundred years of education.

Today, we teach our children the alphabet by first tracing lines. Lines lead to the formation of symbols we call letters. Children begin to recognize that letters form words, then we teach them to read and write those words to communicate concepts. Children first learn to count 1, 2, 3, 4, 5; but it will be a while before they realize these same numbers also represent 12,345. Once a small child first tastes ice cream, he is delighted with the treat. Then he learns there are different flavors of ice cream and he has to choose which flavor he wants. The next time the family goes out for ice cream, his older sister orders a sundae, and he learns ice cream doesn't always come in cones or on sticks. Children 'progress' from one level of understanding to another level when their minds and spirits are ready to glean and absorb the new knowledge they are receiving. It is a process.

FINDING THE BALANCE
We recognized the role parents play in providing their child

a learning environment consistent with the child's developmental age and abilities. By implication this truth speaks to the extremes. That is, overly restrictive environments tend to hold children back from reaching their learning potential but at the other extreme, allowing too many freedoms beyond a child's ability to manage those freedoms creates confusion in the learning process. That is because the child is way out in front of his ability to understand.

Here is the good news. Finding the perfect balance is not all that difficult if you are willing to act on a single universal truth: our lives, world and universe exist because set in place are laws of boundaries. Boundaries! The universe is filled with them, mankind needs them, and children must be taught how to respect them. Boundaries play a role in a pretoddler's life as much as they do in the life of an adult. The psychologist in the opening illustration of this visit decided boundaries were bad. Yet, for those children, boundaries clearly represented the perimeter of security and the outer limits of freedom. Ironically, when the fences (boundaries) came down, the students' freedoms were lost.

Actually this is one of life's interesting paradoxes. If there is any value associated with freedom, it can only be measured by the limitations boundaries provide. Pretoddlers, like most children, will fight the boundaries placed on them, yet thrive within them. Give them limitations and they become creative. In one sense, we give them less and they do more.

When considering the role of boundaries, do not stop at what you allow your child to touch or where you allow him the freedom to play. These are physical boundaries. But there is a second category of equal importance. Neurological boundaries impact how the brain organizes thoughts. Your pretoddler's developing brain sets its own boundaries and establishes it's own limitations. But even this, parents can mess up.

MORE THAN A BUNCH OF NEURONS

Although we touched on this point in our previous book, "*Babywise II*", it is a worthy topic to review when it comes to training children between twelve and thirty-six months. Some parents think they can stuff knowledge into the child's developing brain. As well-intentioned these parents may be, their emphasis is in the wrong place — on knowledge accumulation rather than on developing a healthy infrastructure for learning. Helping to stimulate the formation of an efficient knowledge processing system during the critical fourteen-to-forty month period is a 'must-obtain' goal for parenting pretoddlers.

There is no debate among educational professionals that a child's ability to learn is tied to how the brain organizes information and what stimulates thought, ideas, and answers. This is one reason why a pretoddler's curiosity should not be hindered but rather directed by his parents. To some extent, any activity that engages a pretoddler's interest, attention, or imagination is a type of brain 'fertilizer'. If it provokes a response or investigation, the brain is actively working, growing, and organizing.

'Actively' is used here in contrast to the less-desirable, passive form of learning. An example of passive learning would be sitting too long in front of the television and absorbing too many videos or cartoons. These activities do not help with optimal brain organization, because learning is passive and not interactive, as it needs to be.

Mothers commonly ask "is there really an advantage to reading stories to pretoddlers"? Our answer is, "Yes, of course!" There are many advantages, but not necessarily the advantages most parents think of. Certainly, reading to your pretoddler creates a physical environment of touch and closeness. Often the child is in a parent's lap, finding security there while being read to. The parent is also teaching self-control, encouraging focusing and attention skills, and reinforcing the very productive skill and habit of sitting quietly.

The child's imagination is also being stimulated, and new interests are developed as Mom walks him through story-land, asking questions about what she is reading. Often children's stories possess a moral component, allowing you to teach toddler-age virtues. These are wonderful by-products of reading to your pretoddler.

However, holding a book in your lap and reading, "See the bunny?" cannot be compared with a trip to the pet store or zoo where Mom also says, "See the bunny!" In the world of your child's developing brain, the real thing is better than a thousand pictures when it comes to the organization taking place.

The bunny moves, sniffs with little bobbing whiskers, chews a green leaf, and hops around his cage. The child's brain is interacting far more with the real thing than with a picture. It is not simply a case of more brain stimulation. The type of stimulation facilitates better organization. When the child petted the bunny, more senses were stimulated, including sight, sound, smell, and touch as well as a warm, loving feeling associated with the bunny's furry cuteness.

The walking, talking, touching pretoddler connects better than the sitting, immobile pretoddler. A mobile, exploring pretoddler learns faster and more efficiently than the child whose feet rarely leave the couch and whose eyes are glued to the television screen. The networking of brain activity connecting mobility and discovery is indeed greater than the type of passive learning where there is only data being put into the child's mind but there is no output of energy or stimulation of the senses.

What does this mean for "Sesame Street"? The popular children's program (debuted in 1968) has had a measure of educational success, with an emphasis on repetition with numbers, reciting the alphabet, and teaching limited social skills such as 'cooperation'. It may have served three generations as a great program and entertaining baby-sitter, but it came with a developmental price-tag. What educational television can not do, and will never be able to achieve, is to have a two-way conversation with its young viewers.

A pretoddler and toddler's language formation, for example, does not develop solely by listening. The formation of language must include the interaction of talking back and forth between people. Your pretoddler must have opportunities to talk, interact, and respond rather than just recite. Studio-generated television programming cannot do this. The child that sits for hours in front of a television can only achieve "passive learning". Even if it is the best of the "Veggie Tales", he is still missing half of the equation. The more hours of passive learning and the less opportunity he has to compensate for this type of linear input, the more disorganized the brain becomes, because the responsive side of the brain is increasingly left unattended.

Please take heart. We are not asking you to throw out your television or burn your children's DVD collection or buy a pet rabbit. We are encouraging you to carefully monitor the amount of time your pretoddler spends watching television because a sufficient stimulus for learning cannot be achieved by 'passive' means. Human interaction provides the loving context for learning.

Finding the Neurological Balance

We see two dangers involving the wrong type of stimulation. Too much 'parent-led' stimulation used to enhance a child's intelligence pushes the child too fast and does not allow the brain to absorb the information the child has been receiving. When we speak of "too much parent-led stimulation" we are referring to pushing a pretoddler in an academic sense, i.e. teaching your baby Swahili. Knowledge is piling up because it has nowhere to go.

'Child-led' stimulation is a second concern. When a child is the 'leader' in finding his stimulation, he randomly moves from activity to activity and from toy to toy without any predetermined goal in mind. It is not helpful to allow your pretoddler unlimited freedom of exploration. While his developing brain may receive plenty of sensory input, the overload short-changes the process of association, assimilation, and organization.

Some clinicians suggest the best way to teach children is to allow them to explore at will through trial-and-error in a non-structured environment. When we say, 'trial-and-error', we mean a child will choose something to do with no guidance from an adult. The problem comes because the child has no pressure placed on him to learn, if something appears too difficult at first. The system fails the child because there is no "report card time", meaning there is no expectation to learn because he is not held accountable to learn. This is a bad start to life. The child's learning is only being facilitated not directed.

Facilitating a child's learning and teaching a child are two distinctly different approaches. Facilitators oversee an activity but rarely step in to teach or lead. They are there to 'assist' as needed and allow children to pick and choose what they want to do, hoping they will learn something in the process.

"What does every child really need from his parents?" We believe first and foremost he or she needs an environment suitable for learning and parents who pro-actively direct the opportunities to learn. The home is the child's first learning environment and sets the pattern for attitudes toward people, activities and life in general. Parents are to be the "directors" of learning by creating, encouraging, and managing healthy learning environments that provides wholesome stimuli.

EMOTIONAL RESPONSES

Speaking of wholesome stimuli, let's talk about the boundaries associated with your pretoddler's developing emotions. By way of analogy, consider the common household phone. When they ring we rarely think about the complex network of wires, cables and satellite systems required to make the call happen. The lines coming to your home originate from the phone company's "brain-center" located down line where highly specialized circuitry and switches manage numerous signals. The signals are carried on 'trunk lines' that can send and receive electronic messages simultaneously.

In a similar way, neuroscientists have mapped the 'trunk line' serving the emotional circuits of the brain. Similar to home phone lines, the brain uses the same circuits for sending and receiving emotional messages. But unlike our phone lines, the messages themselves actually build and strengthen the lines ability to understand the message. Sound confusing? Let's bring some clarity to this amazing aspect of building emotionally healthy children.

Your child is playing with his See-N-Say. As he pulls the handle and the dial turns, it produces animal sounds. Your pretoddler laughs with excitement. Hearing your words of affirmation and the clapping of your hands, he turns to see how excited you are on his behalf.

What happened during this exchange? His emotion of joy is met with your emotion of joy. The electrical impulse that created the emotion of joy was reinforced by your response. But what if you did not show any emotion or showed disapproval? What happens then? The impulse controlling the transmission of joy is countered with a completely unrelated impulse. Disapproval or indifference sends a competing signal in this case discouraging the joyful impulse.

Research seems to indicate that if positive emotional signals are not met with similar positive signals, then the power of the first emotion can be suppressed or lost. That means, if your child is joyful, be joyful, if excited about a discovery, be excited with him. In this way, you are encouraging his joy and excitement which will show him the value of those emotions.

The Necessary Balance

Neuroscientists are not telling us to remove the potentiality of all negative emotions from the child's life. Rather we are to reflect back to our children the emotions they display. But there is a necessary balance. The various circuits that establish emotions come through patterns forged and repeated over time. There are some emotions that should be suppressed. Reinforce the right patterns that come from right behavior but do not reinforce the negative patterns of wrong behavior. If your child shows anger, counter with gentle words which often mutts anger. The angry child is often the result of the *anger emotion* reinforced over and over again.

Finally, to bring more balance to the concept of reinforcement, consider the following scenario. Fifteen-month-old

Andrew knocked over the tower of blocks his big brother masterfully created. While this brought forth squeals of glee from Andrew, big brother Matthew is about to seek revenge on the little destroyer. This is not the time for Mom to laugh along with Andrew. She needs to correct him instead. Do not make excuses for Andrew such as, "Oh he is just a baby and didn't mean to do that." Such statements only dismiss the legitimacy of Matthew's feelings. If you laugh when you should be correcting you will really be sending confusing signals to both children.

Chapter Nine
The Funnel Factor

❦

The cognitive ability of a pretoddler and toddler is quite amazing. One way they learn is interaction with their play environment. But there is a developmental caution attached to this statement. Pretoddlers learn best when their play environment or the items they play with are aligned with their developmental age and abilities. That means a child does not learn very much if the play environment or toys around your home are not age-appropriate or in sync with the child's physical or intellectual abilities.

Since learning comes in progressive stages, training should take place in the same way. For this reason, parents need to provide their child with a learning environment that matches new information with the child's ability to understand and assimilate that information. One way to describe this point is to use a handy household tool, a kitchen funnel.

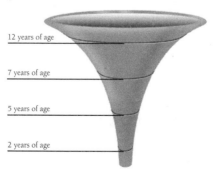

12 years of age

7 years of age

5 years of age

2 years of age

Please note of our funnel diagram. The shape represents a very important parenting concept that from this point forward you will hear us refer to many times, especially as your little one moves into the upcoming toddlerhood transition phase. The long stem represents the early stages of parenting. It's narrow because your pretoddler doesn't possess the ability to manage very much of life outside the stem. He requires a significant amount of adult supervision at this point. The funnel represents necessary developmental boundaries. Manage the boundaries and you manage the child, which means you are pro-actively providing your child with a positive and safe environment where he can grow and learn and that is suited to his age and abilities.

As your pretoddler grows in self-control, he begins to earn freedoms in accordance with his developmental age and abilities. This is a win-win situation for both the child and the parent because there is a consensus in the world of childhood experts that states when a child is at peace with his environment, his learning potential increases, learning disorders decrease, and dysfunctional behaviors diminish. That's good news.

What happens to the child who is consistently placed in a learning environment that is not age-appropriate? That is called 'parenting outside the funnel'. 'Outside the funnel' is a phrase that gives definition to those times when parents allow behaviors that are neither age-appropriate nor in alignment with a child's moral and intellectual abilities.

A Pretoddler with Too Many Freedoms

Will and Cherie were impressed by the abundance of curiosity displayed by seventeen-month-old Julia. They thought if a little freedom is good for a curious mind, certainly offering unlimited freedoms would be even better. As a result, sweet little Julia had the freedom to come and go without guidance, explore without limits, and touch without restraint.

This may sound good on the surface, but when she wandered over to their neighbor's driveway and found a discarded cigarette, she was very reluctant to give up her new treasure. As her panicked Mom worked to confiscate this new delight, a temper tantrum followed. And what about the episode earlier in the day, when Julia crawled behind the bushes in the backyard where days earlier Will sprinkled insecticide pellets? What a scene that was!

At the church potluck, Julia made a charming discovery of discarded cake in the trash. Never mind about the flies hoping to cash in on a meal. Fortunately, her adventure was short-lived, but the price of separating her from the trash can was fought valiantly with screams, kicking legs and tears.

Julia was a curious pretoddler with no boundaries until she crossed the line of legitimate health and safety concerns. When Mom or Dad said "No", she didn't understand why they did not want her to proceed with her exploration because she had no frame of reference to base their objections on. That's because limitations were lacking. All children, even little Julia, need boundaries. It's a shame she has to go through so much trauma before her parents realize this. The restraints in her developing world are unpredictable and always 'suddenly' imposed. Did we mention the time she ran in the street, poked the dog with the butter knife, played in the toilet, ripped pictures out of the family photo album, ran off with Uncle Jim's cell phone, and turned on the fireplace gas burner?

How does Julia perceive parental intrusion in her world of freedom? Confusion and frustration are good words to describe what is going on. The problem began when Julia's parents failed to set age-appropriate boundaries. Will and Cherie were parenting 'outside the funnel'. They should have limited Julia's field of exploration by setting age-appropriate boundaries. They needed to train her to respect those boundaries. Instead, they reversed the process, forcing freedom to give way to restraint. Rather than gradually moving her forward toward increased freedoms, Julia's parents kept bumping her backwards with their constant correction and restraint. That is neither a smart or productive way to parent.

GETTING TO THE HEART OF THE MATTER

To allow a fifteen-month-old child freedoms appropriate for a two-year-old or a two-year-old freedoms suitable for his five-year-old sister is to parent 'outside the funnel'. Such freedoms do not facilitate healthy learning patterns - they only contribute to confusion. Practically speaking, the primary enemy of learning in these early ages creeps in when you allow your child to interact with an environment or with items that are meaningless to his life because they are not age-appropriate, and can:

1. Potentially cause harm to himself

2. Hurt others

3. Cause damage to the item

4. Cause damage to property of others

This happens ninety percent of the time when you parent 'outside the funnel'. Do your own assessment. If you start to see that you are constantly correcting, chasing after your pretoddler, if he throws a fit when you remove an object from his hands, or you find yourself repeatedly removing your child from the same unpleasant situations, these are realistic indicators that you are parenting 'outside the funnel'. Be warned, either you manage your pretoddler's environment or his environment will begin to manage your pretoddler and you.

The goal is to achieve developmental harmony that facilitates learning according to the principle of building "precept upon precept" and "line upon line". Another helpful way to understand this principle is to review the following three developmental equations.

1. Freedoms greater than self-control = developmental confusion

2. Freedoms less than self-control = developmental frustration

3. Freedoms equal to self-control = developmental harmony

The first equation, (which we have discussed at length in this "Visit") demonstrates that freedoms granted to a child that are greater than the child's ability to manage produces developmental confusion. Where does the confusion come in? Like little Julia, developmental confusion becomes part of her day because one minute the freedom to explore the neighbor's driveway is granted, and the next minute Julia's cigarette discovery is taken away. One minute, she is exploring the yard and the next minute she is being removed with urgency from the bushes or fly-infested trash.

Confusing to a pretoddler and toddler? Absolutely! There will be plenty of oppositional tension created because of the nature of the child, so don't create any more opportunities for conflict by not controlling your pretoddler's environment or play items.

Consider the second equation. Freedoms granted that are less than a child's ability to manage those freedoms equals developmental frustration. This equation reflects the opposite extreme. Withholding freedoms from a child who possesses age-appropriate self-control will eventually foster developmental frustration. Instead of too many freedoms and no boundaries, the child is over-restricted and thus not allowed to learn in harmony with his developmental age.

How can you keep life and parenting in harmony with your child's developmental age? What is the center point between the first two equations? The third equation states, "Freedoms granted that are aligned with a child's ability equals developmental harmony." When the environment a child has to play in and his toys are age-appropriate, you're parenting 'inside the funnel'. By doing so, you reduce the need for correction by parenting in harmony with your child's developmental age.

This is what the third equation provides. Harmony! What a beautiful word for the family. The word 'harmony' means, "combining parts into a pleasing and orderly whole." That's exactly what parents should strive to do with their pretoddler. Take the three parts of your pretoddler's day—feeding time, waketime, and sleeptime—and bring harmony to each.

SETTING BOUNDARIES
At this point you are probably thinking, "Now I know why I need to put boundaries in my child's life, but how do I go about it?" To set a boundary means to limit (but not abolish) a child's freedom of: environment, choices, and speech. For health, safety, and moral reasons, setting boundaries denies a child access to something he wants or wants to do. It could be the television remote control, the glasses on Dad's nose, or

THE FUNNEL FACTOR

helping unload the dishwasher. When a child is denied access to something he wants, he will let you know he is unhappy with you. But that is the way it is. How to reinforce the boundaries you establish will be discussed in Visit Four. For now, let's consider some tangible boundaries.

What Can be Used for Boundaries?

To keep your pretoddler from roaming the house, there are things you can use that become boundaries. These things include:

- A pack-and-play playpen
- The high chair or booster seat
- The child's crib
- The Blanket

Using the first items will provide safety preventing him from wandering the house when you are unable to directly supervise his play. For example, a mom is homeschooling her older children and her pretoddler won't stay where she put him. Mom puts him in the high chair and gives him a toy play with. The high chair becomes a boundary for him. Since he is strapped in, he can't go anywhere until Mom gets him out. She might also train to the boundaries of a blanket. This is referred to as "blanket time" and is worthy of your attention. Read more about "blanket time" in Chapter Eleven.

THE MORAL IMPLICATIONS BOUNDARIES

What about the moral component of the funnel analogy and the preciousness of others? When training even a pretoddler you must think of the preciousness of others. The being 'precious' to others starts in the hearts of Mom and Dad. What is this about?

Jim and Brenda were excited about the mobility of sixteen-month old Joshua. Determined not to stifle his joy of discovery they imposed no limits on his exploration. But what happens when the Johnson family visits the home of friends or relatives, or goes shopping, and Joshua touches and perhaps handles everything in sight? How will they restrain him? How will he perceive those restraints?

Parents have a moral/social obligation to protect and honor the property of others and see that their children do the same. That obligation puts more pressure on Jim and Brenda to limit Joshua. Once again we are faced with sudden limitations being placed on a behavior that had no previous limitations. Train in your home as if it were your neighbor's or you too will loose the joy of your visit.

SUMMARY

All parents are obligated to produce a responsible human being, and that challenge should not be left up to chance. Accept the challenges of parenting, realizing that the process of training your child starts with you. As your child responsibly demonstrates age-appropriate behavior and sound judgment, he or she will earn another level of freedom. This type of training results in a developmentally healthy child who is a joy to everyone.

Visit Three
Segment One Summary
The Role of Boundaries

1. Parents must provide a learning environment that is consistent with their pretoddler's developmental age and ability.

2. Precept upon precept and line upon line is a biblical reference to how children learn.

3. Granting play freedoms beyond a child's ability to manage those freedoms creates confusion in the learning process.

4. Overly restrictive environments restrain learning in children.

5. Boundaries at found at every level of the Universe.

6. A play environment without boundaries negatively impacts behavior.

Segment Two Summary
The Funnel Factor

1. The funnel analogy represents necessary developmental boundaries.

2. Parents will either manage their pretoddler's environment or the environment will manage the pretoddler.

3. Children gain freedoms as they become responsible to manage each new level of freedom.

4. When a child is at peace with his environment his learning potential increases.

5. A primary enemy of learning is allowing a child to interact with items that:

    a.   are meaningless to his life,

    b.   can potentially cause harm,

    c.   can hurt others,

    d.   can cause damage to an item, or

    e.   can cause damage to the property of others.

Segment Three Summary

The Three Equations

1. Pretoddlers reach optimal learning when their play environment is in harmony with their developmental abilities.

2. The three developmental equations include:

   a. Freedoms granted that are greater than the child's ability to manage those freedoms equals develop mental confusion.

   b. Freedoms granted that are less than a child's ability to manage those Freedoms equals developmental frustration.

   c. Freedoms granted that are aligned with a child's ability equals developmental harmony.

4. Parenting in the funnel means less correction.

5. Parenting in the funnel encourages contentment.

Visit Three — Questions For Review

1. According to the authors, you cannot move your child into a world of knowledge without first securing what? Explain your answer.

2. Explain the paradox between freedom and boundaries in the life of a pretoddler.

3. What is the difference between active and passive learning?

4. Pretoddlers learn best when what happens in their play environment?

5. What is the primary enemy of learning during the pretoddler phase?

6. What does it mean to parent in and outside the funnel?

7. According to the authors, what is a major cause of developmental confusion?

Section Four

Pretoddler Correction

Chapter Ten

The Preventative Side of Correction

⬥

Children are not endowed at birth with self-control, nor has a pretoddler or toddler lived long enough to know how to make wise decisions. They need guidance. Parents fulfill the role of teacher, leader, and mentor in a process called *training*. Training has a variety of components. At the top of the list is Mom and Dad's example. Beware now and in the future, when it comes to training, more is caught than taught, which means your example forms lasting impressions. Secondly, there is also the encouragement side of training which is always positive, affirming and serves to motivate. The third aspect includes the element of correction, a component as necessary as the first two.

When we refer to 'child-training', we are referring to educating and maturing children in three areas of life. They include training in:

1. Life Skills

2. Health and Safety

3. Matters of the Heart

The emphasis does not end when the pretoddler phase is over. This only marks the beginning of a process that will occur throughout a child's growing-up years.

GETTING STARTED

You will learn very quickly once a pretoddler begins to walk, the necessity for pro-actively encouraging positive behaviors and redirecting unwanted behaviors intensifies exponentially. That is why the foundations of all behavior, acceptable or unacceptable, are laid early in life. Most of our readership enjoys the fruit of their parenting efforts as demonstrated by their child's positive response to his routine and nighttime sleep advancements. Those good sleep habits that you now enjoy didn't "just happen." You trained your baby in healthy sleep. The same is true regarding his playpen time. And now is the time to move to the next level of training as your pretoddler's world expands and his life becomes more complex.

As your pretoddler grows, so also grows his need for specific guidance. Part of that guidance comes by way of encouraging right behaviors and responses and a portion will come by correcting inappropriate behavior. We realize it may be difficult to think in terms of correction at these tender ages. But it is! Correction means to realign or bring back from error. While specific guidance and encouragement keeps a child on track, correction brings him back on track when his little hands or feet wander off to places they should not go. This is why learning the best methods of correction are as important as pro-actively training so less correction is needed. In this visit we will talk about both.

FAITH IN GOOD SEEDS

It was my father who instilled within me the love of gardening. He was the master and I his debtor for passing to me the love of planting, and the anticipatory joy of harvest. My boyhood fascination with gardening has never ceased, nor do the wonderful memories of the one who taught me this way of life. Each time I place a seed into the good earth, I marvel at the probabilities. Some seeds are so tiny you wonder how they can survive outside the safe environment of the package. Yet, I have faith in their power to germinate and my years of experience prove their potential.

To draw a parallel with parenting, we know the seeds of responsible behavior are planted in children in a similar way. It is a matter of faith and confidence knowing the good seeds you start with, small as they may be, can and will bear significant fruit in the future. But to enjoy a good harvest you must first sow good seeds and nurture them along the way. Part of the nurturing process is the encouragement side of training. It would be wonderful if that was all a parent needed to do, *encourage*. But there is so much more to parenting. Like our vegetable gardens, parents have to remove the bad and unwanted weeds, or they will undermine your training.

In parenting the weeding process is called correction. Correction is removing the unwanted behaviors, those little impulses that can choke out your good efforts. We correct our children, because as a mom or dad we desire to give them the best environment to grow in, unencumbered by competing forces that diminish healthy behaviors. Sowing, nurturing and weeding is what parenting is all about.

Since the primary function of child-training is to teach responsible behavior, parents should educate, guide, and emphasize inner growth, personal responsibility, and self-control. The teaching process for parent and child begins early. We educate our children by teaching them what is expected of them. We guide them by encouraging right behavior and discouraging wrong behavior, resulting in personal responsibility. In this way inner growth and self-control, two habits of the heart are formed.

Unfortunately, many parents consider correction to be a means of controlling a child's actions in the moment but they fail to realize it is part of the greater training strategy. When you consider the primary objective of training is to build a firm foundation upon which the balance of life is supported, then parenting is understood in a "tomorrow" context. Like seeds planted, the harvest is not today, but comes in a series of tomorrows.

WHAT COMES BEFORE CORRECTION?

Before we get to our discussion of the various age-appropriate forms of correction (the weeding process), let's work through some preventative strategies that can help keep a pretoddler on the right track. After all, the less the child leaves that path, the less you have to correct him and the fewer tears in life, the better. What components make up the proactive, preventative side of training? We describe them below. Some may seem like insignificant seeds that will never produce beneficial fruit, but they do, when nurtured properly and consistently. Consider the following:

Managing the Transitional Objects

We have all seen young children clutching a soft object, such as a blanket or teddy bear when they head off to bed. These items are known as 'security' or 'transitional' objects. A 'transitional object' is 'something familiar to the child that serves a soothing purpose.' These objects usually become established during infancy and may be carried forward into the pretoddler and toddler months. There is no problem with allowing a blanket or teddy bear to have this role for a child for an extended period of time. But there are some items that need your attention now.

For example, in a previous chapter we introduced the bottle to cup transition and stated it should be made by thirteen or fourteen months of age, if not before. Don't let it become a transitional object. The pacifier can also become one when its use is extended beyond actual need. Each month that passes will make it harder to remove "Mr. Binkie". As a parent of a pretoddler, think about starting now if your child is attached in an unhealthy way to either the bottle or pacifier. Steps to successfully remove the bottle are listed in Visit Two. Suggestions of how to remove the pacifier comes next.

De-Binking the Binky

There are many good reasons for using a pacifier with your newborn. But by six months of age, any need for additional sucking is greatly diminished and the pacifier should have been removed. Maybe you didn't take it away and now your baby is a pretoddler with a 'binky' addiction. Does your child still need it to fall asleep? If so, now is the time to start breaking that habit. While your child will not experience any emotional setbacks when the pacifier is finally removed, you the parent, might end up in therapy over this battle!

Okay, where do you begin? Take a needle and stick a small hole in the tip of the pacifier. This releases the vacuum. It's the vacuum bubble that makes the pacifier enjoyable to suck. When the vacuum goes flat 'Mr. Binky' loses some, if not all of his appeal. If that doesn't work, begin to snip a tiny piece off the front of the pacifier, and over several days, gradually reduce its size until there is little to nothing left to suck on.

If these non-invasive methods do not achieve your 'de-binking' goal, move to the third option. You can either go cold turkey, meaning 'Mr. Binky' is here today and gone tomorrow, or work to gradually remove the 'pacifier' over a period of several days. This is done by restricting the place and time of use, such as only allowing it in the crib. Eliminate the pacifier from naps first and then eventually nighttime. Start with one nap at a time. When your child goes to bed without crying three days in a row, you may take 'Mr. Binky' away at the next naptime. Again, when you reach the three-day mark, take it away during the night.

A word of caution is needed here: do not start what you do not intend to finish. In other words, be united in your goal to remove the pacifier, and have the resolve to see it through to the end.

SOWING WRONG SEEDS
Here is a personal experience offered by a Mom from a recent class. Christy writes:

We have two large plants in our living room. The pots are full of dirt and Jess has eyed them since the moment she became mobile. We decided the plants would stay and we would teach Jess not to touch them. When she began to crawl we taught her "don't touch" and would move her away. Now, at sixteen months, she honestly never bothers them. Once every week or so she'll test the waters by pointing to the dirt around the plant, saying, "Day?" Which to her means "Can I get into this?" Our response is "No" and that is the end of it. We stay consistent with this boundary.

Now, contrast the ease of the plant situation with the disaster on the stairs. When she began to crawl, I would let her "practice" going up one step. She couldn't do it without help, so I never really worried about it. However, as she grew, her mobility created a health and safety concern. We started telling her "No", while moving her away from the steps. But it became a matter of 'too little, too late'. The pleasure of climbing the steps was greater than her self-control. Now, at sixteen months, it's an ongoing issue. We finally put up a gate.

How confusing to a little one! Talk about parenting outside the funnel! As tempting as the dirt in the potted plant must be, she never touches it, because she was never allowed to. I don't think the stairs are any more tempting than the dirt in the pot. I just think we gave Jess clear, consistent boundaries with the plants and none with the stairs. In this area I did not 'begin as I meant to go'. I'll remember this lesson if we are blessed with baby number two. Credit-card parenting is hard!!!

What did Christy mean by 'credit-card parenting? It's simple. You can pay now or you can pay later but with interest. Credit-card parenting is hard on the child and on the parent. This example takes us back to "Visit One" and the stated goals for parenting pretoddlers. Work to maintain your child's behavioral assets and try not to pick up any new behavioral liabilities.

SPEAK YOUR CHILD'S NAME
This concept represents another tiny seed that when planted early and nurtured along the way will produce a wonderful harvest. Make it a point to speak to your pretoddler using his or her name. In the instructing and correcting process, parents tend to direct their pretoddler with specific statements such as, "Place your hands on the side of the highchair", "Don't drop

your food" or "Be patient, Mommy is coming with your food". Can parents improve on these instructions? We believe they can and should.

During the pretoddler and early toddler phase preempt your instructions with your child's name. "Jackson, place your hands on the side of the highchair please" or "Jackson, do not drop your food." Because children are by nature '*me*' oriented, putting their name before your instruction draws attention to the specific task you want accomplished. By calling his name while giving your instruction, you are helping him focus. This is really not a new concept. Think about it. When there is a fun item we want our pretoddler to observe, ("Jackson, look at the balloon," "Amy, look at the butterfly") parents almost naturally begin with the child's name. Parents do this because they want their children to hone in on the specific item. The same natural attraction can be applied to parental instructions.

Why start planting this seed now? Because there are future benefits waiting for you just around the corner when your pretoddler moves into the toddler years. You are not going to do this now but by the time your little one reaches twenty months of age, you will make a strategic shift in how you give instructions. Let's look forward for a moment.

Looking for the "Pause"

As your pretoddler approaches twenty months another step is added to your instructions. You will start with the child's name, followed by a pause. Pause, pause, pause, pause! The pause is everything in this next step. Do not go any further with your instruction without first receiving from your child a verbal response, such as "Mommy" or (when his verbal skills are more developed) "Yes Mommy" and eventually, "Yes Mommy,

I'm coming". Only after you receive the child's response will you proceed with your instruction.

For example, Mom calls, "Ethan". Ethan responds to the call of his name, "Yes Mommy". Mom gives her instruction, "It is time to put your trucks away." In the early stages of parenting, you will want to establish in Ethan's mind your right to be the authority in his life. The instructions you give are secondary to Ethan's willingness to respond to your voice. Get this first, and you usually end up having your instruction followed with far less resistance, if any at all.

You can further help facilitate the process by beginning now to establish the habit of saying, "Ethan, come to Mommy" (especially for pretoddlers, as this provides them a *concrete* destination). When you're face to face with your child, take his chin in your hand, look into his eyes, and then give him your instruction. Keep in mind that training your child to obey is a process and you are taking "baby steps" toward the goal of a well-adjusted and responsive child. If you hope to see the promise of a harvest, nurture the tiny seeds of instruction now. Remember, *'begin as you mean to go'*.

One Toy at a Time

When Jason's mom looked in the Family Room, she saw that many toys had been left on the floor while she was busy doing laundry. It would be natural for any mom's instruction to be, "Jason, please pick up your toys and put them away." But this instruction is to broad for a pretoddler. In this situation, Mom should become specific. Looking at the toys she mentally separates them into categories. "Jason, pick up your trucks please." "Jason, pick up your blocks," and so on. In this way, your instructions are not asking the child to do something that is potentially overwhelming, i.e picking up all his toys. The 'divide and conquer' principle works with instruction as well, making it easier for your pretoddler to understand and comply.

Of course, the bigger problem above came when Jason's Mom allowed him to have too many toy choices at one time. As it was in the babyhood playpen days, pretoddlers learn better with a few toys they can actually concentrate on. With too many options in front of a child, any toy that requires a challenge or is slightly difficult is abandoned for the ease of another toy. Yet, *challenge* is a critical learning dynamic. When challenge is removed, discovery is too often lost. Even toys are to serve learning, not just amusement.

SUBSTITUTION VERSUS SUPPRESSION

This parenting idea relates to an unfolding learning mechanism emerging in your pretoddler's brain. The mechanism is called "curiosity" and is a topic worthy of our attention because curiosity, as a learning force, will be with your child for the next eighteen months and beyond. Sometimes curiosity leads to a safe environment, but it can also lead your child in harm's way. Let's summarize the major points of this drive. What do you need to know?

God placed within mankind a natural sense of curiosity. This is the impulse that drives a child to investigate and explore items of interest or to touch and manipulate things with his hands, only to walk away and revisit it again a few minutes later. This function emerges around the time your little one begins to walk.

Think of this from a pretoddler's perspective. Everything in his unfolding world is new, exciting and worthy of at least a minimal glance. It is the newness of a sound or the function of an object that provokes interest. It might be observing a cord being plugged into an outlet, seeing the colorful magazines on the coffee table, watching the dog lap water from his bowl, or noticing how drawers open and close. Pretty standard stuff for adults, but for a pretoddler, these are adventures worthy of attention and investigation.

So what is it that keeps the child coming back to the same item over and over again? It is the power of *novelty* which is the newness of an item. Curiosity is what draws the child to an object, novelty is what keeps him there. Toddlers explore objects and then turn to other items when the novelty begins to wear off.

When was the last time this happened to you? Do you remember the new car and the amount of time your husband spent driving it those first few weeks? In the first month he washed it more than he washed his old car all of last year. He probably drove places he really didn't need to go. But eventually, his interest began to subside and the novelty of the new car wore off. Today he is back to his normal driving routine and the car desperately needs washing.

The same function of novelty is at work with your pretoddler, but multiplied many times over because everything in his life is new to him. Touching the magazines on the coffee table, or playing in the dog's water dish, or worse yet, the toilet, are all novel to the child and will continue to be items of interest, but they are not appropriate play objects. Yet, the child is continually drawn to them even though he has been told not to touch them. What can a parent do? This is where the training concept of substitution versus suppression comes into play.

Let's define some terms. To *suppress* is to 'deny the child a specific action or access.' To *distract* is an 'attempt to redirect the child to a new activity.' With *substitution*, an 'equally desirable experience is offered' similar to the original one that caught your toddler's curiosity in the first place, but the place and time will be under Mom's supervision.

For example, playing in the dog's water dish produces amusement and laughter for your fifteen-month-old, but it also produces a wet floor, a wet child, and a mess for Mom to clean up. Here is where substitution comes into play. Instead of trying to stop or suppress the novelty of playing in the dog's water, substitute something in its place. Put a similar bowl of water in a mother-friendly location – on the patio floor, laundry room or maybe the garage – and let the child have at it. Do this just before bath time or a diaper change when getting wet is not going to be an issue. For the child, the novelty is splashing in the water, That's why your child is attracted to the bowl. The location is actually secondary to him, but it is primary to Mom. This should only take a few times and the novelty is lost and the child is no longer attracted to the dog's water dish.

Of course, you may be thinking, "Why not move the dog's dish and put it up on the counter, removing the temptation altogether?" That is an option and there are items that you will want to remove rather than have them become a point of conflict. But you cannot rearrange your entire home.

Jenny's Kitchen Cabinet Fascination

When Jenny, the Ezzos' youngest daughter was a pretoddler, she was fascinated with the lower kitchen cabinets and drawers. It seemed Mom and Dad were forever removing her from the kitchen when curiosity began to overwhelm her. One day the Ezzos found a solution. Instead of suppressing Jenny's fifteen-month-old curiosity, they allowed her access to one drawer in the kitchen. There they placed pot holders and some small plastic measuring cups. When she started to head to any other cabinet she was easily redirected to play in 'Jenny's drawer'. This lasted off-and-on for a week or two. The novelty of the drawer wore off, Jenny's curiosity was satisfied and she moved on to explore something else.

TODDLER PROOFING: YES OR NO?

Once your pretoddler's legs can take him where his mind directs, it is time to seriously be thinking about setting some boundaries. This includes limitations as to what areas and items are off-limits to his exploring hands and what he can and cannot touch. Will your child understand the 'why' behind your instructions? Of course not! At this point of his development he does not possess the capacity to understand what "No" or "Don't touch" means.

During the process of growth and development, physical achievements gained are usually accompanied by a corresponding increase in understanding. When a pretoddler is old enough to walk, he has the corresponding capacity to discriminate between what he can and cannot touch. That last statement brings us to the next topic - should you 'baby-proof' your home, or 'home-proof' your baby? Which one is best for you and which is best for your child? In the overall scheme of parenting philosophies 'baby-proofing' is relatively new, emerging during the 1970's when traditional parenting practices were being challenged by new theories in child development.

Prior to that decade, most parents 'home-proofed' their children. 'Home-proofing' means 'setting appropriate limitations' on your pretoddler's mobility, introducing freedoms only when your child is old enough and wise enough to understand how to handle them. Where does the difference lie between 'home-proofing' your child and 'baby-proofing' your home? It lies in philosophy.

'Home-proofing' has an ethical dimension that views child-training as a social and moral obligation that goes beyond a child's momentary pleasures. As such, parents should train their pretoddlers with an 'otherness' sensitivity. They realize the self-control instilled in their child at home regarding items that are off limits is the same self-control that makes the child a blessing in the home of others. The opposite is also true. Until a child learns how to respect items in Mom and Dad's living room, he should not have the freedom of exploration in someone else's home.

In contrast, 'baby-proofing' has parents rearranging their living area so the child is never placed in a situation where Mom or Dad would have to limit his freedom of exploration or confront him with the feared words, "No, don't touch." Actually, parents can take comfort in knowing their pretoddler will do just fine with the words "No," or "Do not touch." Saying "No" to your mobile pretoddler or placing reasonable limitations on his exploration will not destroy brain cells, damage his self-esteem or cause him to drop out of school. Think of "No" for what it really is — the furthest extreme of "Yes." "No" doesn't abolish freedom, but only draws a line of safety for the welfare of the child.

CAPACITY AND TRAINING

Your pretoddler is about to enter another long transition, one that will take him from a world of *me, myself* and *I* (dominant during his first two years of life), to a world of understanding that other people, and their property have equal significance. This is the world he will live in for the rest of his life. It seems reasonable then, to 'begin as you mean to go'.

It is generally accepted among the "*On Becoming Babywise*" alumni that pretoddlers have the capacity for some limited self-governance. When faced with the temptation of playing with Dad's beautifully displayed fishing magazines or redirecting his hands, redirecting can win out. But how do you get your pretoddler to that point? As we just mentioned, instead of rearranging your entire home, train your pretoddler in what he can and cannot touch.

Of course there will be many times when your mobile pretoddler will reject or strongly oppose your reasonable instructions. This usually happens because he doesn't know your instructions are reasonable. But train you must. This requires three things.

<u>One</u>: Healthy discipline is always consistent! The child who is corrected consistently when he or she fails to obey is better adjusted than the child whose discipline is inconsistent or incomplete. Consistency keeps you at the right point at each stage of development. Inconsistency creates too many variables for the child to handle, forcing you to do more parenting outside the funnel. When parents reduce or eliminate variables that are not age-appropriate from their child's environment, they establish right learning patterns more quickly and firmly. Order facilitates healthy growth; unlike excessive freedom, which leads to developmental confusion.

<u>Two</u>: Be ready to utilize one of the four corrective strategies explained below. During the pretoddler phase however, you

might consider adding a hand clap to bring attention to your "No". The clapping of your hands will not only draw the child's attention, but also add emphasis to your instruction. Parents also use the sign for "Stop" to get their child's attention. If you are so inclined, even an attention-getting swat on the hand will get the message across, especially if the child is touching something he knows he is not supposed to. For some children this will work faster than any other form of correction. The swat does not have to induce pain, but it must get his attention sufficiently to discourage his actions. The traditional practice of spanking is not appropriate for these young ages. (More on this in the next chapter.)

Three: Be prudent and wise. If you have a valuable or dangerous item, don't take a chance with it. By all means remove it. Secure your bookcases to the wall and place 'knick-knacks' and other fragile items out of reach. It is important that you make your pretoddler's play environment safe, but you don't need to strip your living room of everything as suggested by 'baby-proofing' advocates. If you do that, your child will never learn how to properly interact with those items or attain the levels of self-control that comes with early training.

While there will be times when parental resolve must win, pick your battles wisely. For your sake, and to avoid frustrating your child, do not make his play world too big. If your son develops a fondness with the toilet seat in the guest bathroom, shut the door and keep it closed. We promise, you will have plenty of opportunities to train your pretoddler with items in the living room and kitchen.

Chapter Eleven
How to Pull Weeds

W e now move from the preventative side to the corrective side of training — weed pulling! Your little
one will cross the line. When it happens, what
will you do? Since healthy discipline tries to develop internal
management by educating a child in life principles, there will
be times when parental insistence is necessary. You must learn
how to control situations on behalf of your pretoddler until
he is old enough, wise enough and experienced enough to
control his own life. This is a gradual process that will take
years to accomplish.

There will be many times when your pretoddler will ignore
your safety warnings or instructions. For example, you instruct
your thirteen-month-old not to stand in the highchair, but he
does it anyway. There are two influences at work here. Your
child's misplaced confidence in his desire to stand in the highchair and his inability to understand you have a vested interest
in his safety. What should you do? Start working with basic
restrictive commends.

A thirteen-month-old can understand simple statements
such as "Stop", "No", "Do not touch", or "Do not move". These
are usually the first restrictive commands of early parenting.
But the power is not in the directives; it is in the amount of
parental resolve behind them. To bring meaning to these words:
"Stop" must mean stop, "No" must mean no, "Do not touch"

must mean do not touch, and "Do not move" must mean do not move. The sooner parents begin to work toward age appropriate compliance and obedience, the faster your child learns the intent behind your instructions.

By obedience, we don't mean a child yields as a result of repeated threats, bribes, or manipulation from his parents. Worse than these methods is that of adult persuasion. You cannot govern your pretoddler by a persuasive argument. Your pretoddler is a pretoddler, not your moral or intellectual peer. Attempting to reason with a thirteen-month-old is not commendable. Lead, direct, and guide him in the confidence of your wisdom.

THE CONSTANT VERSUS THE VARIABLES

As with many aspects of child development, there are both constant and variable influences to contend with. Parents are the constant influence on training. Whether at mealtime, or playtime, parents should maintain a constant level of expectation regarding their child's behavior. For example, the instructions, "Do not drop your food" and "Do not touch the stereo," differ only in the nature of the activity, not in the level of parental expectation. The 'variable' is 'the place or manner of offense', but the 'constant' is 'the level of expectation'. The "No" of the highchair should be the same as the "No" of the living room. Although the settings and activities vary, when parents say, "No", their expectation should not.

Look for the Root

When a behavioral challenge emerges at mealtime, consider other conflicts that may have taken place during the day. Are they related? Is the problem tied only to food, or does the child act similarly in other settings? If your son is having trouble keeping his hands where they belong at mealtime, is he also struggling with touching off-limit items in the living room? If so, the root problem is a general lack of self-control and not exclusively a mealtime issue. Of course a lack of self-control at this age is fairly normal and should be expected. But remember, one of your goals is to instill a healthy sense of self-generated self-control so your child will emerge in a few years with this virtue well established.

METHODS OF CORRECTION

As a parent, you are an active participant in your child's process of learning how to put thoughts into action. It isn't wise to delay training, hoping the process will get easier later on. Dealing with a problem 'later' usually means backtracking. Make this your parenting motto – "Train, don't retrain! No credit-card parenting."

In the pretoddler phase of development, behaviors needing correction are initially wrong functionally, but not morally. By that we mean pretoddlers do not possess the capacity to know right from wrong any more than they know their left hand from their right hand. At this age, they learn right from wrong based on Mom and Dad's response to their actions.

A pretoddler's age limits the methods of correction that can be applied with effectiveness. (This will change in a few months.) Here are the most common methods applied with routine success.

1. <u>Verbal Correction</u>: This speaks to the 'tone and intent'. It is what you are saying and how you are saying it. One key component to setting boundaries for your mobile pretoddler

is instilling a right response to your instructions. The goal is to train the child to your voice (which includes tone and modulation), and not to the object. The tone of a verbal correction needs to be firm. Yelling at your child is not correcting him. He is more than likely not even listening to what you are saying because of fear. A parent's voice can be firm and calm at the same time. Your voice and tone represent authority to your child. Use them wisely.

2. <u>Isolation:</u> 'Removing the child from an act or place of conflict.' A crib, playpen or highchair (when rolled to a quiet place) can be used to isolate a pretoddler. Some parents wonder if a pretoddler will start to associate the crib with a place of punishment. Will this affect his or her naps or nighttime sleep? To both questions, the answer is, "No!" Your pretoddler knows when he is there to sleep and when he is there to get self-control. The factors surrounding isolation are different from those surrounding bedtime. The hugs and kisses associated with bedtime are noticeably absent when he is in isolation. Parental behavior is what cues the child as to what is going on, not the crib itself.

3. <u>Logical Consequences</u>: This includes 'losing the privilege' associated with a toy or item. The child that drops his toys on the outside of his playpen will learn soon enough that they do not come back. The purpose of logical consequences in pretoddler training is to draw attention to his actions and/or your instruction.

4. <u>Discomfort</u>: Discomfort tends to 'get attention' faster than anything. A squeeze on the hand, even a swat for wiggling on a changing table, when accompanied by verbal correction acts

as a deterrent to wrong and health-threatening behaviors. Using such methods for the express purpose of calling attention to a boundary will not leave your child psychologically scarred, affect his self-esteem, or teach the child violence. But it will instill a healthy sense of self-restriction. As stated, spanking, as traditionally practiced in our society, is not an acceptable form of correction during the pretoddler phase of development. If it is to be introduced into the life of your child at all we recommend it be done much later, sparingly and always in moments of calm and love, never in our out of frustration.

AVOIDING POWER STRUGGLES

Can a thirteen-month-old pull a parent into a power struggle? Yes! Many do it every day. A power struggle results when a parent fails to exercise his or her authority wisely. That is, they allow themselves to be forced into a 'must win' situation over a seemingly minor conflict. There will be some early parent-child conflicts when parental resolve must be victorious, but you should choose well which hill you're willing to 'die' on. Wise parenting is superior to power-parenting.

Here is a true-life example of how a minor conflict can turned into a serious battle of the wills. The portable heater was off-limits to Matthew's hands. When he touched it, he received a verbal warning from his Mom. Undeterred, he began to play with it again. This time Mom went to Matthew, took the offending hand in her hand, squeezed it, and sternly said "No". He immediately touched it a third time and then a fourth. Back and forth they went. Matthew's mom was now into a full-blown power struggle with a fourteen-month old child. If she gives up, Matthew learns that persistence pays off and obedience is optional. If she continues, both she and Matthew will be exasperated setting the stage for more challenges next time.

What can a mother do? There is a way to defuse the potential power struggle and maintain the integrity of your parenting. First, realize as sweet as your little one is, he or she possesses the capacity to battle you in stubbornness. Second, using the above example, Mom in this case could have simply picked Matthew up and isolated him to his crib or moved him to another room after the first or second warning. In either case, she would have wisely exercised her parental authority and not allowed herself to get into the power struggle. Such actions would achieve her goal without compromising respect for her authority and without manipulating the environment.

Surrendering with Dignity

A pretoddler will often continue in defiance when a parent makes the option of surrendering intolerable to him. That is, he will persist in wrong behavior when a parent fails to provide room for him to surrender with dignity. This is how conflicts flare into power struggles. And yes, this can and does happen even with a thirteen-month-old who has determined he is not going to give in.

To demonstrate this point, we'll return to Matthew and the heater. When Matthew's mom battled him toe-to-toe, her very presence made surrendering to her authority difficult, if not impossible. If she had walked away from him after her second warning to stop touching the heater, he most likely would have left the heater alone because he no longer had an audience. Mom's presence extended the conflict. By leaving, she would have given him room to surrender with dignity, rather than face a continued challenge. If Matthew doesn't leave the heater alone after Mom leaves, then removing him to the crib for isolation will be the best option. That's wisdom parenting. The dignity of your child should always be persevered, even in correction. Correct graciously.

SUMMARY

Healthy discipline consists of a number of essential principles and actions, some encouraging, some corrective. The encouraging side for the pretoddler includes affirmation, praise, and rewards. The corrective side consists of verbal reproof, allowing logical consequences to come and run their course, isolation, restrictions, loss of privileges, and discomfort to the hand with a squeeze. Both encouragement and correction has purpose, meaning, and a legitimate place in the overall learning and training process. Over the next six to eight months, strengthen that foundation and expand on it. Be thinking to the future while enjoying today. Much of your success during the toddler years will be a result of what you're doing now. The long-term results of right training are wonderful.

Chapter Twelve
The Pretoddler Topic Pool

Your child has just celebrated his first birthday and each month from this point forward brings new challenges and more questions. Our goal in presenting this information is to help the reader better understand a pretoddler's expanding world. We know when understanding increases, wisdom follows. Wisdom leads to confidence in your parenting when dealing with unforeseen or unexpected changes that come your way. The topics include:

- Bath Time
- Blanket Time
- Community: How Important is it?
- Dental Care
- Learning Activities
- Socialization/Play Groups
- Speech Delay
- Structure and Routine
- Tantrums
- Timer Benefits
- Toys and Tots

- Thumb Sucking
- Why 'Actions Precede Beliefs'

BATH TIME

While pretoddlers do not need a full bath every day they should receive a sponge/washcloth bath at least once a day. Most moms find this to be adequate, alternating between a full and partial bath every second or third day.

When bathing a pretoddler, safety is a primary concern. Consider the following safety tips:

1. Monitor the water level in the tub. Four to six inches of water is more than adequate.

2. Do not allow your pretoddler to play with or even touch the faucets. Accidentally turning on the hot water can lead to burns.

3. Make it a rule that he is not allowed to stand up in the tub and see that your pretoddler obeys that rule.

4. Although your pretoddler is highly mobile and able to sit upright without difficulty, do not leave him unattended. You may not think that drowning is possible at this age, but it is. In addition he may attempt to get out of the tub by himself which could lead to a serious injury.

5. While you might have siblings bathing together, a preschooler with a pretoddler is not a substitute for Mom. Do not leave them unattended. Playful siblings do cause injury.

6. When washing your child's hair, continue to cover his eyes with your hand or washcloth as you rinse his head. Look for shampoos that are manufactured specifically for children.

Most pretoddlers love their bath time so add a few play items, like plastic cups, boats or ball and take a few moments to make this a fun time and an activity your pretoddler looks forward to. Some Moms schedule bath time as a specific morning waketime activity. Others see it as a soothing and fun way to wind down the day just before bedtime. Adding non-allergic lotions and a gentle rub down after the bath aids the process of winding down. And one last word of encouragement. Bath time is a great activity for Dad to get involved with.

BLANKET TIME

Everyone was more preoccupied with the little girl in front of the bleachers than what was happening on the soccer field. Observing in amazement, they watched while two and-a-half year old Brooke played contently within a three by three foot square drawn in the sand by Mom. The toys today were improvised and included a small stone, two sticks and a leaf. Brooke sat and entertained herself for forty-five minutes, just long enough to allow here older sibling to finish his game. How did Brooke's mother get her to play so contently without wandering away from her make shift play area? It started during infancy when Mom began to introduce Brooke to blanket time.

Blanket time provides an opportunity to teach a child to play in a limited area without a physical parameter. Ideally, you should have started this during the babyhood transition. If you're starting late, you will have to be specific in your intent to have some blanket-time training opportunities, a couple of times a day. When you begin, start with 3 to 5 minutes with your child playing with a few toys. In time this can be extended up to thirty minutes.

When training, stay close to your child because the likelihood of him moving off the blanket is great. When he does you must immediately return him to the blanket with instructions to stay put and play with his toys. There is only one thing that will keep him there and that is Mom or Dad's resolve to do so. This is more than training in self-control, it is training in obedience and both will have their rewards in the coming months.

Use the timer for blanket time just as you do for playpen time. When the timer goes off, make a big deal of his accomplishment, "blanket time is over", then move onto the next activity.

Blanket time has present and future benefits. It can easily be moved anywhere in the house or on the back patio, or even to a location in the yard. Where you will really enjoy the fruit of your training are those occasions when you are away from home, such as at the doctor's office, sibling sporting events, or visiting with friends or relatives. Brooke's story speaks of greater future benefits when your training pays wonderful dividends. How many times have you been surprised when your five-minute meeting turned into an hour? Travel smart! Why not keep a bag in the car with a blanket and a few toys that will come in handy for those surprise situations. You never know when that quick trip might turn out to be longer than expected.

Blanket time is not something limited to just the pretoddler phase. Plan on using this right through the toddler years. Even at two years of age, Mom will still be making most of the choices regarding which toys are appropriate. Be wise about those choices. For example, you might give your son some blocks and cars together to provide an opportunity for his imagination, allowing him to build bridges and roads to drive his cars over. Don't worry about having to change out toys frequently; certainly the same toys for a week will help a child learn to play with what has been given him.

COMMUNITY: HOW IMPORTANT IS IT?

Community can mean many things to many people. We use it to refer to a group of families sharing common interests, values, and a significant commitment to an ideal for the mutual benefit of the individual and the collective membership. In other words, to quote 'The Three Musketeers', "All for one and one for all!"

Why is it important to have a community? When parenting gets tough, and it will, it helps to be part of a team striving towards a common standard that will support and encourage your efforts. It's within your community that friendships are forged, play-groups are formed, and parental accountability is framed. Your *Babywise* friendships provide a great opportunity to foster such relationships. These are the other moms and dads whose hearts and minds are already in sync with yours. They can make up and strengthen your likeminded community, providing support to your family and parenting efforts.

DENTAL CARE

Early evaluation and education is the key to preventing many dental diseases, and a good start is very important! Ideally, your child should have visited the dentist around the time his first tooth broke through. If this didn't happen, now is a good time to make that "well baby dental checkup." At that visit, your child's risk for decay is evaluated and you will be provided literature and techniques to clean a pretoddler's teeth. Your dentist can advise you if your child requires fluoride supplements. This is especially important because many children today have meals and drinks prepared with bottled water, which typically contains no fluoride. Even a balanced diet does not guarantee adequate fluoride to prevent future decay. Fluoridated water is important. It has been shown to be very safe and effective in reducing a child's risk for decay.

Unfortunately, severe early childhood decay is a public health problem and children are often brought to their first dental visit because a tooth begins to hurt. A first visit to the dentist under these circumstances can be traumatic on the child and straining on the parent. This can be very straining on both the child and the parent, as extensive treatment may be needed. Such traumatic experiences may have ramifications into adulthood. Many patients refer to a 'bad' childhood experience as to why they do not go to the dentist regularly as adults.

Cleaning and Preventing Tooth Decay

You should have begun cleaning your child's teeth after the first tooth appeared. Cleaning was very simple back then, a wet wash cloth rubbed gently against the teeth was all that was needed. Now you will begin to transition to a toothbrush.

Before using toothpaste, consult with your dentist. If you and your dentist decide to use toothpaste, make sure to use only a "pea" sized amount. There are two reasons for this. First, the primary years is an important developmental period for tooth development. Over use of fluoride can cause damage to the tooth enamel. Second, pretoddlers have a natural tendency to swallow toothpaste. Ingesting toothpaste may be too strong for little tummies when consumed in excessive amounts. This is also a good reason to keep your toothpaste well out of reach of your toddler.

Remember, the 'baby' teeth are a necessary gateway for the permanent teeth. If they are lost prematurely it can have a negative impact on the eruption of the permanent dentition. Therefore, starting habits early like good home cleanings, limiting juices and snacks, and regular visits to your dentist are simple keys to unlock lifelong oral health for your child. Studies have shown, that when children develop the habit of good dental care early, they tend to carry those habits into adulthood. You can find more information from the American Academy of Pediatric Dentistry website.

LEARNING ACTIVITIES
In the pretoddler months improved motor control makes it possible for your son or daughter to engage in new types of play activity. Some activities challenge present skill levels by placing demands on your little one for a solution. It's the challenge in such cases that stimulates learning. Here are some activities that will enhance the process of learning.

• Much of a pretoddler's discovery is possible because of improved hand-eye coordination. Helping your child develop this coordination can be encouraged by spending time with him working with blocks, post and ring toys, and containers with lids. These activities also encourage logical thinking through the building and matching process. Do not overly assist in any of the tasks, just suggest and encourage. If the child hands you a lid, hand it back while encouraging him to put it on the container you point to. If you see him becoming repetitively frustrated, perhaps this portion of playtime should be over.

• In regards to language development, a pretoddler will begin to use a language that has meaning only to himself. We have all heard toddlers babble. They are actually saying something, what no ones knows and that may be a good thing. Many children use 'sign language', but not always in the way we intended when we first began teaching her sign language. For example, at fourteen months, your daughter signs "All done" when you put green beans on her plate. This is not exactly how the "All done" sign is meant to be used, but it works for her.

The point is, language and vocabulary formation is critically important to life in general. The intimate relationship between vocabulary and thought is one of the greatest influences on reasoning powers.

Talk, talk, talk to your pretoddler, while feeding, playing, dressing, walking or riding in the car. Use adult language, not baby talk. Read to your child everyday. Stimulate your pretoddler's memory skills through games like peek-a-boo and patty-cake and practice waving "bye-bye". Put words into your child and concepts will come out.

• Filling the airways of your home with classical music as a way of providing an educational edge to infants and toddlers, is another topic of contemporary interest. Playing music around young children has become known as the "Mozart Effect". This was based on a study done in 1993 which suggested that listening to Mozart could increase one's spatial reasoning (aiding logic). But hang on. Before rushing out to pick up CDs by your favorite classical composer, understand the research was done on college students and not infants or pretoddlers. Although the research was not thorough, the findings had some qualified value.

Music is a unique language because it has the ability to completely bypass the listener's mind and speak directly to the heart. We know that classical music is very orderly in its construction and can convey a peaceful spirit. Man has the ability to listen to music on two levels. On the surface we hear the song and melody. Below the surface, but just above the subconscious level, we hear the logic of the melody.

It is theorized that when young children are exposed to classical music, the logic center of the brain is strengthened and those areas dependent on logic, (mathematics and complex reasoning skills) are reinforced. While there is some evidence supporting this conclusion, we wish to point out that none of it is linked to music videos or flashing images coming from a television screen. If classical music is not your first choice, consider filling your home with instrumental or praise music.

SOCIALIZATION/PLAY GROUPS

To preface our comments, let's start with this truth: Preschools and day-care provide a necessary service to families where both parents must work outside the home. In most cases, preschool staffers are dedicated and caring individuals who hold children's best interest at heart. We have friends around the country who operate wonderful day-care centers, where love abounds and understanding of unique needs brings satisfaction and a sense of relief to parents who otherwise would choose to be home with their child.

In these cases, the necessity of placing a toddler in an organized educational setting is *good* because it meets the immediate need of a working couple. *Better*, might be to find a likeminded relative or friend to care for your child in a home setting. *Best* we believe finds Mom home with her children. Why do we believe that? Because aside from Dad's, there is not another pair of hands more perfectly fitted to the heart of your child than your own.

While we acknowledge that the ideal is preferable, we also recognize that is not possible in all cases. Thus, we wish to approach the topic of children, socialization, and preschool strictly from a developmental perspective. Our commentary should not be construed as a social statement on the rightness or wrongness of preschools or daycare. We are writing on this topic because every family is different and the variables of each family will not allow for cookie-cutter solutions when it comes to the necessity of child care.

At the same time we must work with the reality of each situation. For example, the Mom who works outside the home will face different challenges in parenting at the end of the day than a stay-at-home Mom. Some of her parenting goals will not be achieved quite as fast. But when it comes to who is the "better Mom", between the two scenarios, the good news is this: The venue in which your child spends his day, whether at home or at school, is not a true measurement of your parenting. Remember back to *Babywise* when you were confronted with the breast or bottle feeding decision? Descriptive terms such as "more caring" or "better" could not be attributed to one over the other in that case. The same is true of parents who work outside the home. As authors, our duty is not to pass judgment on those who have no other option but day-care, rather it is to provide understanding to those who do have an option and to help couples understand that "good" is not "better" and "better" is not "best". When it comes to socialization, what is best for children when options are available to parents?

Preschoolers and Socialization

There is a utopian theory suggesting mankind can engineer the perfect socialized child. This scary thought usually has some preschool component attached to it. The very nature of children wars against the notion that a formalized preschool experience can gain a child a social advantage that he otherwise could not have obtained. Any discussion about socialization must start with the nature of children. Pretoddlers and young toddlers are too ego-centric to be placed into an environment filled with other ego-centric children. When you put ten pretoddlers in a room, whose intrinsic worldview is centered on "*me, myself and I*" you cannot expect them to emerge with a healthy sense of others. Most studies concur with this point of view.

The danger of pushing a child into early formalized socialization is that it works against the child's developmental age, abilities and interest. Pretoddlers right up to their second birthday engage in self-play not cooperative play. If you place three eighteen-month old children in the same room, with similar toys, their natural inclination is to self-focus to the point of turning their backs to the other children and playing by themselves. No social interaction will take place except when one child desires a toy that another has in his possession and attempts a 'hostile takeover'. Socialized play, where there is give-and-take within an activity usually begins around the age of three, rarely before.

Pretoddlers and toddlers placed in organized preschool are often negatively impacted by the peer pressure associated with children from homes that do not share your values. That is because pretoddlers and toddlers tend to imitate negative behaviors such as bullying, physical aggression, pushing and taking toys from others more easily than they internalize virtuous conduct such as sharing, cooperating, and kindness. This happens regardless of the wonderful efforts of the teacher.

Do you recall our earlier comments relating to emotions needing reciprocal responses? Pretoddlers lack the ability to empathize and thus cannot provide the reciprocal affirmation needed. They simply cannot turn off their sense of "*me, myself and I*" and become other oriented. This is why over-socialization causes children to become too reliant on receiving approval and affirmation from a peer group, rather than from the steady and unchallenged source they find in their own home.

Parents hoping to give their children an educational advantage must realize that research is fairly consistent when it comes to academic gains. If there be any advantage gained from pushing children into preschool modules, it does not last much beyond the second grade. When you compare the temporary advantage gained with the offset in emotional and social setbacks, you have to ask if outsourcing your child is best for his development.

A better alternative to a formalized preschool setting is scheduling playtimes with other pretoddlers in your home, or your child in the home of others who come from families of likeminded persuasion. One playmate once or twice a week is plenty for the first couple of years of life. Children fair better socially when they experience pleasant contacts with other children, (even on a limited basis), than children in preschool settings where peer socialization is not always pleasant.

The belief that by placing a child in preschool will cause him to come out the other side socialized and better adjusted, speaks to the power of advertising more than it does to sound principles of socialization.

SPEECH DELAY

As parents, we look forward to hearing those first words from our child. But what if your sixteen-month-old says fewer words than the kids in your coffee group? Is he falling behind? Should you be worried? Out of the Ezzos' six grandchildren, two of them were delayed in speech, yet the same two walked very early compared to their cousins. Is there a correlation here? Probably not! The developmental fact is: some kids walk early and some don't. Some kids talk early and some don't. In the situation with the grandchildren, the speech centers kicked in around eighteen months and within few months of that, their vocabulary was on pare with their cousins.

The onset and development of speech patterns is influenced by genetics and fostered positively or negatively by the home environment. Too many videos prior to the second birthday tend to delay speech development while healthy and purposeful adult communication directed toward your pretoddler encourages it. Unless there are other factors going on with the child's development, most pediatricians will tell you not to worry if your child is not using words or many words by sixteen to eighteen months of age. This is not considered outside the 'normal' range of development, although it is something you should keep track of. The tricky part for any health-care professional is deciding whether there is actually a problem or just an immaturity in the speech-center of the brain.

By twelve-to-fourteen months of age, most kids are making sounds, babbling and possibly using single word nouns such as "Momma", "Dadda", and "baby". Between fourteen-to-eighteen months of age, the vocabulary begins to grow upward to twenty or more words. Keep in mind that during the process of vocabulary building, your child will understand more than he can say. We bring this to your attention so you do not use your pretoddler's lack of words to measure whether or not he understands your basic and simple instructions, such as "Don't touch".

If there is a concern regarding your child's speech, a trained professional will usually inquire as to whether your child:

- Responds to sounds at all, such as laughter, a dog barking or music
- Has difficulty understanding simple questions or requests such as "All done?", "Give Mommy a kiss", "Wave bye-bye"
- Is using sign language but not speaking words
- Relies on pointing gestures, grunting or screaming more than words
- Does not demonstrate basic pretoddler skills such as waving "bye-bye" or clapping his hands when excited

Whether you suspect a problem or not, there are some speech enhancement activities that should be part of your day. They include:

- Speak words to your child throughout the day. If you're taking a walk, point to and name the butterfly, flower, colorful buds or the red bird in the tree. While in the store, name the various fruits and vegetables and funny looking seafood. While preparing his meal, tell him how much he is going to enjoy his breakfast. Be specific by naming the items being prepared. Make happy sounds with him, "Yum" and encourage him to mimic those sounds.
- Talk, sing and encourage with simple words like "Dadda", "Mommy", "puppy" or the name of his siblings and grandparents.
- Reading to your child should be the utmost priority using

age-appropriate books with plenty of pictures to point to.

• Again, avoid using 'baby talk'.

STRUCTURE AND ROUTINE

For whatever reason, parents who greatly benefited from having their baby on a routine, give it up when their children start walking. Pretoddlers love predictability and established patterns for mealtimes, wake-times, naps and bedtime. Learning opportunities should predominately be the result of planning, which is much easier when you have a consistent routine. These learning opportunities include:

1. Structured playtime alone

2. Times with family members

3. Free playtime

When planning your pretoddler's daily routine, work in ten to twenty minute increments (or whatever you feel is appropriate for your child). Most pretoddlers at the younger end of the transition find it hard to sustain interest in an activity much longer than that. Your eventual goal is thirty-minutes per activity.

Structured Playtime Alone

This is a specific time during the day when your child has time to play by himself. It starts in the early months with 'play-pen and blanket time' eventually moving to 'room time' in the toddler phase. The following are skills children learn when they play alone:

• Mental Focusing Skills

- Sustained Attention Span
- Creativity
- Self-play Adeptness
- Orderliness

We encourage you to use the playpen (pack-and-play) as long as your child will happily stay in it. The playpen or blanket should be in a place where you can easily check on your child. Stay with it until your child is ready to move to roomtime.

Time with Family Members

It is important to enjoy your relationship with your pretoddler, but you must find the right balance between playing with your child and becoming a source of entertainment for him. If you find that your child clings to you, refuses to go to Dad or his siblings, and cries when you leave the room, it is likely he has too much playtime with Mom. He is over attached! Not over attached relationally speaking but over attached to being amused by you. Be purposeful to schedule time for your pretoddler to spend time with each member of the family.

Free Playtime

Free Playtime does not mean you allow your pretoddler to roam the house looking to entertain himself. Rather, it refers to planned and impromptu times when your child plays with his toys at a play center. A play center is a small, safe area containing a basket or bin of age-appropriate toys that he can go to and choose what he wants to play with. This is an important distinction. In 'Structured Play Time', Mom chooses what the child will do. In 'Free Play Time', the child gets to choose.

When play is over, help your child with the task of cleaning up. By directing him to put some, if not all of his toys away, you are teaching him that playtime is not over until the toys are picked up.

TANTRUMS

Because pretoddlers have not achieved a consistent or satisfactory level of self-control to handle disappointment or frustration, they cannot be expected to display emotional maturity when they get upset. While there are acceptable ways of dealing with disappointments, throwing temper tantrums is not one of them.

The propensity for throwing temper tantrums is normal for pretoddlers. That is not to say tantrums should be ignored or allowed, just expected. As your child continues to develop self-control, the potential for tantrums will decrease. But the self-control we speak of is not gained overnight. Meanwhile, you still need to deal with the unpleasantries of the here and now. Be consistent in dealing with your child's tantrums and you will see them disappear.

What can parents do?

<u>One</u>: Take note of when and where your child throws his fits. Is it only in public, just before or after a meal, or when he is tired and in need of a nap? Your awareness of any pattern may help to prevent tantrums before they happen.

<u>Two</u>: Look for early signals your pretoddler gives before he throws a tantrum. Does he whine when he doesn't get what he wants? We know of a pretoddler who moved his arms back and forth along the sides of his body before he lost control.

We worked with another little guy who would grunt when he didn't get what he wanted. He would point to the object or ask again, and if the answer was still "No", then he would throw a fit. Put your child in his crib to get self-control at the first sign, and the tantrum won't follow.

Three: As difficult as it may be, try not to talk your pretoddler out of his tantrum. Without realizing it, you are encouraging the behavior by rewarding it with attention. To be effective, a child's tantrum needs a sympathetic audience. Your attempt to be an understanding parent in this moment is not a help because talking provides the audience he wants. Parents, if your child is at the point of throwing a tantrum, he is not listening to anything you say anyway. So stop talking.

Four: Use isolation for temper tantrums. Deposit the child in his crib until he has calmed down.

TIMER BENEFITS

The use of a timer is very beneficial when first starting any new activity that requires your child's cooperation and can be carried all the way into elementary school. Whether your child adapts with perfect calm or cries in protest, your goal is for him to associate the end of the activity with the timer. Otherwise, he will begin to think if he cries long enough and loud enough, "Mom will come get me". When introducing a new activity, start with five minutes on the timer. If he is showing interest and wants to play longer, add more time. You can always add time again, but once you have set the timer, you should not take time away.

TOYS AND TOTS

The pretoddler months represent a critical period in the development for your child. The activity of play helps promote optimal learning because the many forms of play interact with repetition, memory, motor skills and hand-eye coordination. Toys are a big part of this. How can a parent know how to select toys suited to their child's developmental age and their wallet? Here are some guidelines to consider.

Guidelines for Choosing a Toy

<u>One</u>: Safety considerations will always be at the top of the list, regardless of your child's age. When it comes to pretoddler toys, look for small parts, edges, projectiles, and other potential dangerous pieces that can break off or cause injury. Make sure any painted toys are labeled 'non-toxic' paints. In most cases, a toy that requires constant supervision is not age-appropriate. Many parents buy toys based on the box or packaging. Open the box and evaluate the contents for yourself.

<u>Two</u>: Imagination is a tool of the mind. Hours of imaginative play come about with everyday items we adults so quickly discard. Look around your house. A 2 x 4 plank of wood cut up into blocks, patches of colored fabric, an empty tea kettle, or those throw-away plastic plant pots can all find a purpose in your child's developing imagination. All parents need to do is use a little imagination. A child will create uncommon adventures with common household objects that toys purchased in stores could never produce. You will be amazed at the hours of play a pretoddler can have with a cardboard box he can crawl into. Fun items are waiting to be discovered. Just make sure they are safe!

<u>Three</u>: Is the toy challenging and stimulating without going beyond the child's skill or maturity level? Most toys provide a recommended age-range on the packaging. Parents should pay attention to the guidelines. However, if you think a toy is too advanced for your child even though he fits into the age-range listed on the box, trust your own judgement about this. The age recommendations are guidelines.

<u>Four</u>: Beware of fads. There are many toys available today based on children's movies and cartoon series. It will be a while before your pretoddler has a superhero, so save your money. Your child doesn't care if he has the latest 'Spiderman' pillow or doll.

<u>Five</u>: Is the toy durable? Toys that are easily cleaned, repaired, and reused year after year give you the best value for your money. Ask yourself, "Will the toy last longer than the box it comes in?" If you suspect it won't, don't buy it.

<u>Six</u>: For pretoddlers, all toys should be child-powered. If a toy that uses batteries and a toy that doesn't are next to each other on the shelf in the store, opt for the one that your child must manipulate and power himself. A child-powered toy requires children to engage physically and mentally, which stimulates creativity with the toy. For the most part, battery-powered toys require adult supervision, which limits when the child can play with it.

<u>Seven</u>: Does the toy have long-lasting 'play value'? Blocks are a good example of this. A toy should hold a child's interest and interaction for many months and not just for a few minutes.

<u>Eight</u>: What type of emotional response are you getting? Look

for toys that result in happy dreams and a healthy soul. We would recommend that you stay away from toys rooted in fear, such as monsters, ghouls, ghosts, goblins, or gross-fantasy creatures.

THUMB SUCKING

Children, whether, infants, pretoddlers or toddlers suck thumbs and fingers out of habit more than a deep seated psychological need for comfort. Children find thumb sucking soothing during times of stress, fatigue and calm. Unlike the pacifier that can be removed, the thumb is physically attached to the child and the child is emotionally attached to the thumb. Statistically, fifty percent of infants give up thumb sucking on their own by six or seven months. But if you have one that falls on the other side of those statistics, keep reading.

What can a parent of a twelve-month old do about thumb or finger sucking? Not a whole lot! Unlike the pacifier you can't poke a hole in it to release any vacuum nor can you snip the edge of it until there is nothing left. Yet someday, it will have to be brought under the governance of self-control. And it will. But when?

The pleasure of thumb sucking is not something your pre-toddler is likely to give up. Why should he? He is not motivated by social stigma from peers, (because he really doesn't have any), nor is he capable of understanding the casual relationship between thumb sucking and future orthodontic work. The only thing he knows is "right now this satisfies me."

What are some things parents can do to discourage thumb sucking? Hold on to your hats, our straight talk advice is: If your pretoddler enjoys the pleasure of his thumb or fingers, don't worry about it now. Thumb sucking is an extension of a natural reflex, not an adapted behavior. There is no developmental issue associated with it that mandates an immediate fix. There are no health and safety concerns nor is it going to affect the alignment of his permanent teeth. (That becomes a greater issue if a five-year-old is still sucking his thumb.) It is not a moral issue governed by values of right or wrong. It is simply a childhood pleasure issue carried over from infancy.

Our recommendation is to apply passive pressure if you wish, or wait until he at least has the ability to voluntarily cooperative in the process. This might mean waiting until he is three years old. (By then it might be gone.) Why wait? At three and certainly by four he can better relate to your instructions and should have the self-discipline necessary to cooperate with you in bringing the habit under control.

Does this mean you shouldn't make any attempts to discourage thumb sucking? We wouldn't go that far. You can start now by gently removing the thumb from his mouth while saying "No thumb now." This is passive pressure. But we wouldn't make it a battle during the pretoddler phase. You have more important issues to deal with. There will always be a pyramid of behavioral concerns that must be brought under control through obedience training during the pretoddler and toddler years. Simple commends such as "Stop", "Don't touch" "Come to Mommy" "Stay on the Blanket" are at the top of the pyramid. Insisting on full voluntary compliance with thumb sucking, in our opinion is ranked much lower on the pyramid of concern.

If you haven't already established the "when" or "where" thumb sucking can take place, certainly by ages of two and-a-half or three you can begin to impose such limits. For example, you might direct your child to sit on a chair or his bed if he is going to suck his thumb. Obedience to these instructions is far more important than the thumb sucking itself.

Between the ages of three and four definitely start the "step process" of elimination. This is a gradual approach that may span a month or two. First, start by limiting your child's freedom to suck his thumb any place or any time. He now only has the freedom to suck his thumb in his room. After a couple of weeks tighten the parameter by only allowing thumb sucking while sitting or lying down on his bed. This restriction is followed by only at naptime or nighttime. Eventually he will only be allowed to suck his thumb at night in his bed. If you get to this point, thumb sucking will soon be a thing of the past.

WHY ACTIONS PRECEDE BELIEF
We conclude this section, (and series) with a fundamental *truth* of development most relevant to the successful future of your parenting. The truth is: *in childhood, actions precede beliefs, but in adulthood the opposite is true, beliefs precede actions*. What are the parenting implications of this fact? You step into a scene in which a child snatched a toy out of the hand of another leaving the other child in tears. Then you hear: "Oh, he is to young to understand that was wrong." Maybe he is. But if that was your child what would you do? Dismiss it or correct it?

When parenting through the pretoddler and toddler months, your primary training emphasis is actually on outward behavior, not necessarily matters of your child's heart. That means you will be helping your child become familiar with right actions even though he may be years away from fully understanding the moral implications of his behavior.

That is because children under two years-of-age act out of their *natures* and not from a moral sense of right and wrong. They clearly demonstrate a capacity to *do wrong*, but do not have the capacity to understand, *why it is wrong*. Regardless of that fact, correction is still necessary. Correction establishes the *habits* of the heart until the knowledge of right and wrong (beliefs) take over. From the living room we move to a highchair example. The fact that your child has no moral understanding as to why food should not be intentionally dropped from his highchair does not mean you hold back instruction or restriction. By all means correct.

Months ago, you began teaching your pretoddler how to sign "please". Today, he uses the please sign routinely even though it will be a couple of years before he fully appreciate the courtesy the word "please" represents. Will you stop requiring him to sign "please" because he doesn't understand the moral qualities of the word? We trust not. We train our children to do the right actions and restrain wrong behavior long before they are able to understand why right is right and wrong is wrong. Actions in young children precede beliefs.

The complexity of child training will multiply ten-fold when your pretoddler finally crosses the bridge to toddlerhood. Knowing that fact, we leave you with this final reminder: Do not hold back training thinking you must wait until your child is old enough to understand right from wrong before encouraging him to do right and to avoid wrong. If you delay this training in the pretoddler months, behaviorally speaking, you will be playing catch-up throughout the toddler and preschool years. *Begin as you mean to go*. Manage your assets and minimize your child's behavioral liabilities. Enjoy the journey through the pretoddler phase.

Visit Four

Segment One Summary
Nurturing Good Seeds

1. Be careful not to encourage the growth of any seed that will have to be "weeded out" at a later age.

2. Transitional objects are common items children carry into the next phase of development.

3. The pacifier and bottle are two "transitional objects" parents should work on eliminating from their pretoddler's day.

4. Staying consistent with your boundaries pays positive behavioral dividends during the day.

5. Include your pretoddler's name when giving instruction.

6. Employ the practice of "substitution" instead of "suppression".

   a. To suppress is to deny the child a specific action or access.

   b. To substitute is to offer an equally desirable experience in place of what the child is doing.

7. Remember to keep your child's play environment age-appropriate.

Segment Two Summary
Forms of Pretoddler Correction

1. Direct and redirect with your voice tones.

2. Utilize an attention getting hand squeeze.

3. Defining training options:

   a. To *isolate*: removes the child from a challenging circumstance.

   b. To *distract*: redirects a child's attention.

   c. To *redirect*: is to point a child in another direction.

5. Teach your pretoddler consequences by removing items he should not be touching.

6. Physical correction, such as a swat may become appropriate toward the end of this transition.

7. Remember, the best form of correction is prevention.

Segment Three Summary
General Review

1. Remember every child is different and every family unique; not all desired behaviors are achieved at the same time.

2. Stay mindful of the parenting goal.

3. Focus on not losing any ground with your pretoddler; by not losing ground you are actually gaining ground.

4. Do not underestimate the speed in which your pretoddler advances in cognitive skills.

5. Coming up next: *On Becoming Toddlerwise.*

Visit Four — Questions For Review

1. What is the thinking behind the use of speaking your child's name when giving instruction?

2. Please define the difference between the parenting concepts of: *suppression, distraction* and *substitution*:

3. In training a pretoddler, the four restrictive commands are "Stop", "No", "Do not touch", and "Do not move". To bring complete meaning to these words, what must happen?

4. Please name and briefly describe the four methods of corrective discipline for pretoddlers.

   a.

b.

c.

d.

5. What is a power struggle and can it happen with a pretoddler?

Index of Terms

More Parenting Resources

ON BECOMING BABYWISE

Coming with the applause of over two million parents and twice as many babies worldwide, *On Becoming Babywise* provides a prescription for responsible parenting. The infant management plan offered by Ezzo and Bucknam successfully and naturally helps infants synchronize their feeding/waketime and night-time sleep cycles. The results? You parent a happy, healthy and contented baby who will begin sleeping through the night on average between seven and nine weeks of age. Learning how to manage your newborn is the first critical step in teaching your child how to manage his life.

ON BECOMING BABYWISE II

This series teaches the practical side of introducing solid foods, managing mealtimes, nap transitions, traveling with your infant, setting reasonable limits while encouraging healthy exploration and much more. You will learn how to teach your child to use sign language for basic needs, a tool proven to help stimulates cognitive growth and advance communication.

ON BECOMING PRE-TODDLERWISE

Between the ages of twelve and eighteen months, a pretoddler is on a one-way track to the future. This is a growth phase made-up of tiny transitions linking the fading babyhood days with the up coming toddlerhood months. It is a time when your child is in neither. *On Becoming Pretoddlerwise* deals with a specific right of passage and the corresponding challenges parents will face.

ON BECOMING TODDLERWISE

By eighteen months of age, the child emerges into a period of life know affectionately as the Toddler Years. How ready are you for this new experience? The toddler years are the learning fields and you need a trustworthy guide to take you through the unfolding maze of your child's developing world. *On Becoming Toddlerwise* is a tool chest of workable strategies and ideas that multiplies your child's learning opportunities in a loving and nurturing way. This resource is as practical as it is informative.

ON BECOMING POTTYWISE FOR TODDLERS

Potty training doesn't have to be complicated and neither should a resource that explains it. *On Becoming Pottywise for Toddlers* looks to developmental readiness cures of children as the starting point of potty training. Readiness is primary perquisite for successful training according to best selling authors, Gary Ezzo and Pediatrician Robert Bucknam. While no promise can be made, they can tell you that many moms successfully complete their training in a day or two, some achieve it literally in hours. This resource is filled with time test wisdom, workable solutions and practical answers to the myriad of questions that arise during training.

ON BECOMING PRESCHOOLWISE

Who can understand the mind of a preschooler? You can! Know that above all else, a preschooler is a learner. His amazing powers of reasoning and discrimination are awakened through a world of play and imagination. The growth period between ages three and five years is all about learning, and *On Becoming Preschoolwise* is all about helping parents create the right opportunities and best environment to optimize their child's learning potential. From teaching about the importance of play to learn-ing how to prepare a preschooler for the first day of school, from organizing your child's week to understanding childhood fears and calming parental anxiety, sound advice and practical application await the reader.

ON BECOMING CHILDWISE

Equip yourself with more than fifteen Childwise principles for training kids in the art of living happily among family and friends. Foster the safe, secure growth of your child's self-con-cept and worldview. *On Becoming Childwise* shows you how to raise emotionally balanced, intellectually assertive, and morally sensible children. It's the essential guidebook for the adventur-ous years from toddler to grade-schooler!

ON BECOMING PRETEENWISE

The middle years, eight to twelve years of age, are perhaps the most significant attitude-forming period in the life of a child. It is during this time that the roots of moral character are established. From the foundation that is formed, healthy or not-so-healthy family relationships will be built. These are the years when patterns of behavior are firmly established pat-terns that will impact your parent-child relationship for decades to come. Rightly meeting the small challenges of the middle years significantly reduces the likelihood of big challenges in the teen years. In other words, the groundwork you lay during your child's middle years will forever impact your relationship even long after he or she is grown. Included are discussions related to the eight major transitions of middle years children including how to create a family-dependent and not a peer-dependent child. How to lead by your relational influence and not by coercive authority. What discipline methods work and what methods do not work and how to recognize if your child is in trouble.

ON BECOMING TEENWISE

Why do teenagers rebel? Is it due to hormones, a suppressed primal desire to stake out their own domain, or a natural and predictable process of growth? To what extent do parents encourage or discourage the storm and stress of adolescence? *On Becoming Teenwise* looks at the many factors that make living with a teenager a blessing or a curse. It exposes the notions of secular myth and brings to light the proven how-to applications of building and maintaining healthy relationships with your teens. Whether you worry about your teen and dating or your teen and drugs, the principles of *On Becoming Teenwise* are appropriate and applicable for both extremes and everyone in between. They do work!